"There are very few thing[s]  Christian, my faith is at th[e] native, Alabama football i[s] a tremendous job bringin[g] Christian that knows on Saturday, 'Roll Tide' is used to say just about anything."

—Dr. Matthew Dunaway, PraiseFest Ministries

"I moved to Alabama in the early 1980s, a Tennessee alum who grew up as a Georgia fan and have witnessed the intensity of the fans in the Alabama-Auburn rivalry. It is a source of identity for football fans throughout the state and beyond. But, while fans may identify with their favorite team, there is a higher identity, and that is a Christian's identity in the Lord. Del Duduit takes memorable Crimson Tide moments and blends them together with truth from God's Word in a guide that can help people think a bit deeper about lessons from the gridiron."

—Bob Crittenden, host, *The Meeting House,*
Faith Radio in Alabama

"This book is full of Alabama football history and thoughtful insight from Scripture. Bama fans will enjoy reading these excerpts from past games and the devotionals that follow. The rich history of what makes the Crimson Tide legendary is clearly seen here. I'll be giving this book to my Bama friends and loved ones!"

—the Tibbs family, Hoover, Alabama

BAMA BELIEVER

40 DAYS OF DEVOTIONS FOR THE ROLL TIDE FAITHFUL

DEL DUDUIT

IRON STREAM
BOOKS

An imprint of Iron Stream Media
Birmingham, Alabama

Other books in the Stars of the Faith Series

Dugout Devotions: Inspirational Hits from MLB's Best
First Down Devotions: Inspiration from NFL's Best
Auburn Believer: 40 Days of Devotions for the Tiger Faithful

Iron Stream Books
100 Missionary Ridge
Birmingham, AL 35242
IronStreamMedia.com
Iron Stream Books is an imprint of Iron Stream Media

Library of Congress Control Number: 2020934661

ISBN-13: 978-1-56309-368-5
Ebook ISBN: 978-1-56309-369-2

1 2 3 4 5—24 23 22 21 20

This book is dedicated to all Roll Tide fans and those who appreciate good football and faith.

CONTENTS

ACKNOWLEDGMENTS

Several people played key roles in making this book a reality. I would like to thank the following for their efforts in bringing *Bama Believer: 40 Days of Devotions for the Roll Tide Faithful* to you.

- ➤ My wife Angie for being the initial editor of this book and for her support.

- ➤ My agent Cyle Young for his work to get it in front of the right publisher.

- ➤ My publisher John Herring for his trust in me.

- ➤ My associated publisher Ramona Richards for her encouragement.

- ➤ My final editor Reagan Jackson for her wonderful eye and making this book better.

- ➤ My production crew and cheerleaders, Meredith Dunn and Tina Atchenson, at Iron Stream Media.

- ➤ My Lord and Savior for this exciting opportunity.

DAY 1
MAKE A GOOD IMPRESSION

November 4, 1922: Alabama 9, Pennsylvania 7

All Scripture is breathed out by God and profitable for teaching, for reproof, for correction, and for training in righteousness. —2 Timothy 3:16

Southern-style football was not respected in the early twentieth century. In fact, it was not considered serious competition by major college football powerhouses like Pennsylvania, Harvard, Yale, and other teams in the northeast.

Alabama started the season 2–2–1 while the Pennsylvania Quakers boasted an undefeated 5–0 mark at the time.

The Crimson Tide rolled into Franklin Field in Philadelphia as the underdog, but the team was fresh off a big win over Navy. This was the second home game for Pennsylvania on its newly renovated field.

Sportswriter Grantland Rice predicted a 21–0 thumping of Alabama at the hands of Coach John Heisman's squad. The Tide was not considered a worthy opponent and was not to be taken seriously.

The hype fueled the Crimson Tide as Coach Xen Scott's team held its own throughout the game.

Pennsylvania fans knew something was up when their team only led 7–3 going into halftime.

Alabama quarterback Charles Bartlett orchestrated a drive that resulted in the game's only touchdown in the third quarter and boosted his team's lead to 9–7.

From there, the Tide defense rolled and controlled the Quaker offense.

Alabama stunned the football world and sent a message that Southern boys knew how to play football.

It didn't take long for word to spread to Tuscaloosa where fans set bonfires to celebrate the upset win.

Bartlett later was named honorable mention as a Walter Camp All-American.

The next week, the Tide knocked off Louisiana State 47–3 and finished the season 6–3–1.

Alabama football was for real, and everyone was now aware.

That the man of God may be complete, equipped for every good work. —2 Timothy 3:17

FAITH AND PRIDE

You have a chance every day to make an initial and lasting impression. Whether you are at a job interview, your first day at work, or your fiftieth visit to your favorite coffee house, someone will meet you for the first time. What will they think of you? Will they see you being rude to a waitress? Will they observe you cut in line or watch you leave without paying your bill? Perhaps they might overhear you saying negative words on the phone or complaining about your spouse. No matter the situation, how you present yourself matters.

AND ROLL TIDE

No one is on their game every day. There might be times when someone might see you in anger or observe you in the heat of the moment that does not match up with your true personality. It happens. This is why it's so important for you to strive to demonstrate the kindness and gentleness you need to display as a believer. This does not mean you allow the world or people to walk over you. It does, however, suggest that you let your light shine to attract others to the joy you have in your heart. Here are some tips and suggestions to keep in mind on your daily journey after you break the huddle and head out the door:

➢ Smile: A grin can be contagious and a fantastic way to start a conversation. If you smile and demonstrate joy in your heart, others who may not have it might ask you why you do this all the time. When you smile—no matter the situation—mercy comes your way. "Make your face shine on your servant; save me in your steadfast love!" (Psalm 31:16).

➢ Dress Well: Your outward appearance may lead to certain perceptions and can impact your reputation. Most likely you try to look your best when you go to a job interview because you want to impress your potential employer. You should also care how you look when you meet people in your daily journey. You don't have to wear your Sunday best on vacation or on the golf course, but you should try to have a clean and respectful appearance wherever you go if possible. There are circumstances in life that call for a relaxed appearance, but take pride in yourself. Avoid going to Walmart in your pajamas. When you dress in a shabby fashion, people remember the clothes. When you make an effort to look presentable, they remember the person. Be memorable for the right reason.

➤ Show Gratitude: Say thank you with sincerity to the people you come in contact with every day. This might be a server, a cashier, or a bank teller. This piggybacks what I said earlier about smiling—show an attitude of gratitude. Be humble and grateful for your blessings, no matter the size. "You will be enriched in every way to be generous in every way, which through us will produce thanksgiving to God" (2 Corinthians 9:11).

➤ Listen: When you speak with people, make sure you pay attention to them and respect their time. If you go to lunch with a friend who has a problem, lend an ear and keep quiet. Let them know you care, and don't try to top their stories.

➤ Be Genuine: No one likes a person who is fake. Greet people with a firm handshake and make eye contact. This lets them know you are for real and not just going through the motions. The secret to success is authenticity. Be the same person in the gym who shows up in the boardroom or in the pew at church. "A wicked man puts on a bold face, but the upright gives thought to his ways" (Proverbs 21:29).

Alabama's upset of Pennsylvania served notice that the team was to be taken seriously. From that moment forward, the Crimson Tide has earned respect from everyone in college football. Play by the rules and take steps to be a godly person to distinguish yourself as someone who is admired for your morality, character, and principles.

DAY 2
THE START OF SOMETHING GREAT

January 1, 1926: Alabama 20, Washington 19

In the morning sow your seed, and in the evening do not withhold your hand; for you do not know which will prosper, either this or that, or whether both alike will be good. —Ecclesiastes 11:6 NKJV

The momentum was building, and the time was right.

Alabama produced an undefeated regular season and was headed to face the mighty Washington Huskies in Pasadena for the Rose Bowl championship.

However, the matchup almost did not happen because the Rose Bowl committee sent out an initial invitation to Tulane University. The Green Wave declined the invite because they felt they would get wiped up by the bigger Washington squad.

Bring on the Tide, who was not afraid but instead jumped at the chance to play for the title.

Washington put on a show in the first two quarters and led 12–0 at halftime.

But Alabama came out and fired on all cylinders, whipping off twenty points in the third quarter.

Fullback Pooley Hubert plunged into the end zone from one yard out for the first score.

That was followed by a fifty-nine-yard touchdown catch by Johnny "Mack" Brown from Grant Gillis.

7

Brown, who was named the Rose Bowl MVP, also hauled in a thirty-yard touchdown from Hubert to give the Crimson Tide a 20–12 lead. (He would later go on to achieve fame as an actor.)

Washington managed to score a touchdown in the final quarter, but the Bama defense sustained the lead through the end of the game, and the 1926 Rose Bowl jump-started the school's championship run and football dominance.

> Go to the ant, you sluggard! Consider her ways and be wise. —Proverbs 6:6 NKJV

FAITH AND PRIDE

Have you been sitting on the sidelines wanting a chance to do something big for God in your life? The responsibilities that come with maturity, such as landing a job or beginning a family, are tough challenges. Demands of the daily grind can dictate your time. Deep down, you may have a desire to be a productive member of the Lord's team. You know you have talents and abilities, but restraints on your time can leave you exhausted at the end of the day. Where do you find time? How do you begin?

AND ROLL TIDE

You have made the decision to answer God's call and do more for Him. But you still have important obligations to your family, church, and employer. You don't want to become so overwhelmed that you can't get anything done. There are many ways to maintain balance in your life and serve your Heavenly Father. Here are some tips to help you break the huddle and do more for God:

Day 2: The Start of Something Great

➢ Be Specific: When you pray, ask God for His will in your life. Thank Him for all He has done for you, and tell Him the desires of your heart. Ask Him to open doors and allow you to perform His work. This doesn't mean to ask the Lord for the winning lottery ticket number. For example, I wanted to begin a writing ministry and asked God to lead me down the appropriate path. He connected me with the right people, and my dream happened because I was willing to sacrifice and do what He instructed. "You ask and do not receive, because you ask amiss, that you may spend it on your pleasure" (James 4:3 NKJV).

➢ Be Excited: When you do something new, there is always a sense of excitement and curiosity. When you take a vacation, you explore and find out interesting things about your destination. Treat your newfound desire to serve Him in a different capacity with enthusiasm.

➢ Be Patient: When I begin to write a chapter in a new book, I know it's going to take time to complete it. I research and make sure my facts are right and allow the process to take shape. A friend of mine operates a ministry that hosts three events a year. This may seem small, but the work and the planning that goes into these three events is staggering. Be patient and keep moving forward.

➢ Be Thankful: Show gratitude for the blessings God has given you. Give Him praise and thank Him for His protection, mercy, and grace. We deserve none of it, but He is so good to love and care for His children no matter how big or small our problems may be.

➢ Be Effective: Now get to work. When I was given some advice on how to begin my writing ministry, I got it done. Have the same attitude that Johnny "Mack" Brown had in the Rose Bowl game. He went out with his underdog team and won the game. The win won't just fall in your lap, and there are always obstacles to overcome. But you have to get off the sidelines for it to happen. "For whatever is born of God overcomes the world. And this is the victory that has overcome the world—our faith" (1 John 5:4 NKJV).

When Tulane turned down the invitation to play Washington in the Rose Bowl, the door opened for Alabama, which exhibited a different attitude from the Green Wave. They viewed it as an opportunity to show the world what Crimson Tide football was all about. Today is your day to do the same.

DAY 3
PRACTICE MAKES PRAYER

January 1, 1931: Alabama 24, Washington State 0

Rejoice always, pray without ceasing, give thanks in all circumstances; for this is the will of God in Christ Jesus for you. —1 Thessalonians 5:16–18

The Crimson Tide was invited to Pasadena to battle Washington State in the Rose Bowl.

Alabama coach Wallace Wade maintained a strict and vigorous practice routine that even included working on Christmas Day.

There was limited sightseeing and no Tournament of Roses parade for the players.

They were in California for one reason—to win a National Championship.

Coach Wade had a system, and it worked for the undefeated Crimson Tide. He started each game with the second string on the field.

He did this to get a feel of what the other team would do, and it also used up the energy of the opponent's starters.

In this case, the strategic move paid off as the first quarter ended with no score.

The first team went into the game to start the second quarter, and Coach Wade kept his plan of keeping the ball on the ground.

Effective punts kept the Washington offensive pinned deep in its own territory.

Then it was time for the air attack.

Jimmy Moore, a receiver, went into the backfield and took the handoff only to throw it to John Suther for a thirty-nine-yard touchdown.

On the next possession, Moore once again fired a pass, this time to Ben Smith, who romped to the one-yard line. The next play, quarterback Jon Campbell plowed into the end zone.

But the Crimson Tide was not finished. Campbell galloped forty-three yards for a score, and the team boasted a 21–0 lead at the break.

At the start of the second half, Coach Wade stuck to his plan, and the second string saw the field again to begin the third quarter.

By the time the contest was over, the Tide rolled to a 24–0 beatdown of Washington State to win the Rose Bowl.

Wade made sure his players were prepared and practiced for this moment.

He did not let the attractions of the festive Rose Bowl distract his players. They were there to win.

Continue steadfastly in prayer, being watchful in it with thanksgiving. —Colossians 4:2

FAITH AND PRIDE

How much do you pray each day? Are you distracted by the daily parades of obstacles in your home? Are you disciplined enough to stick to your game plan and hold devotions on a regular basis, no matter what is going on around you? This can be difficult to do, but you must focus on your time with the Lord in prayer.

AND ROLL TIDE

Just like the game plan that defeated Washington State in the Rose Bowl, you too must develop a strategy to keep the forces of evil at bay in your own life. The key to success is a commitment to prayer. Other factors come into play like reading your Bible and going to church. But prayer is your main line of communication with God. When you slack off on your prayer life, you will begin to tumble the ball and lose field position—just what the enemy wants. Satan wants nothing more than to pin you deep in your own territory and sack you for a loss on third down. But drop back in the pocket of protection and fire at the receiver who is wide open downfield. Here are five tips to enjoy a Rose Bowl prayer life:

➢ Keep It Simple: The Lord wants you to praise Him from the heart. You don't need long-drawn-out words. Thank Him for His blessing on you and your family, and tell Him how much you love Him. Remember to thank Him for what He's already done for you before you ask Him for the desires of your heart.

➢ Be Intentional: Just like you stop in for your morning coffee at your favorite shop, your prayer time should be a strict part of your routine. You always manage to keep your tee times or your appointment to get your hair cut—why not set it on your mental clock to talk to God every day at the same time? Morning is the best time to spend with God before the day's business can make you lose your focus. "Whatever you ask in my name, this I will do, that the Father may be glorified in the Son" (John 14:13).

➢ Limit Distractions: Turn off the television, put down the cell phone, and tune everything else out. Treasure your time alone with the Creator. He deserves your full attention.

➢ Make It Impromptu: Time with God is not only at church or during your set-apart study and prayer time. You could find yourself stopped in traffic or on the shore fishing with your children. Take a minute to whisper a quick prayer and thank Him for all your blessings. Your spouse appreciates an unexpected hello from you, and so does your Heavenly Father. "Then you call upon me and come and pray to me, and I will hear you" (Jeremiah 29:12).

➢ Engage: When you go to lunch with a coworker or dinner with your spouse, you give them your full attention. The same is true when you genuinely seek His face. You can confide in the Lord with your problems and share your hopes and dreams. Make Him your best friend. He listens and understands and knows what is best for you. "The Lord is near to all who call on him, to all who call on him in truth" (Psalm 145:18).

Coach Wade knew his players could be distracted by the pageantry of the Rose Bowl, and he made sure they were not. His practice routine never wavered, not even when they were in a different element. No matter where you are in life, make sure you keep to your game plan and talk to the Lord every day.

DAY 4
BE PATIENT AND GROW IN GOD

January 1, 1935: Alabama 29, Stanford 13

And let us not grow weary of doing good, for in due season we will reap, if we do not give up. —Galatians 6:9

A new era dawned in Alabama under Coach Frank Thomas.

He guided the Tide to an undefeated season and back to the prestigious Rose Bowl in Pasadena, California.

Alabama football had earned a solid reputation as a college football powerhouse.

Now the team was looking to grab its third Rose Bowl win and, more importantly, its third national championship.

But prior to the matchup with Stanford, there was some controversy.

Many experts thought Minnesota deserved the tap to go to the Rose Bowl since they were undefeated, but Big Ten Conference rules at the time did not allow its teams to play in post-season games.

Alabama now had something to prove once again.

More than 84,000 people crammed into the stadium to watch the two teams square off for the title.

The Crimson Tide got off to a slow start and trailed by a touchdown at the end of the first period.

The offense sputtered until Coach Thomas unleashed the passing game.

That opened up Alabama's running attack, and Millard "Dixie" Howell romped sixty-seven yards for a touchdown, increasing the lead to 16–7.

The second quarter was the beginning of an onslaught as the Crimson Tide rolled for twenty-two points in the period.

Stanford could not recover, and Alabama won 29–13 to claim another National Championship and begin the establishment of a football tradition.

But something was brewing in the Alabama locker room.

There was a player on the team with the name Paul "Bear" Bryant.

His legacy was just starting, and his time would later come.

For I know the plans I have for you, declares the LORD, plans for welfare and not for evil, to give you a future and a hope. —Jeremiah 29:11

FAITH AND PRIDE

You might be a new believer in Christ and are not sure what direction your life will take. Or perhaps you have been following the Lord many years and have wondered when He is going to answer your prayers. Maybe you struggle with financial issues or job insecurity. You know you have talent, but the right door has not opened for you.

AND ROLL TIDE

Waiting on God's timing can be nerve-racking for all of us. As humans, we often try to take matters into our own hands. But time and again, the Lord always comes through. His plan is always worth waiting for, and it is much more creative than anything we could ever envision. He always delivers, and we should expect great things to happen when we pray in faith, believing that He sees the complete picture and knows what is best for us. Here are some tips to consider while you wait on God's timing:

➤ Be Thankful for Any Trial You Face: When you go through a challenging situation, you will go stronger if you turn it over to the Lord. Surrender to His will and let Him guide you. And always give Him credit and praise in the storm. "Praise the LORD! Oh give thanks to the LORD, for he is good, for his steadfast love endures forever!" (Psalm 106:1).

➤ Don't Get Ahead of the Holy Spirit: This is perhaps the hardest part. Often when people want something to happen so badly and it doesn't, they want to take control. Too many times, this is a mistake, and you miss out on the story God can write for your life. He always knows what's best for us. "Be patient, therefore, brothers, until the coming of the Lord. See how the farmer waits for the precious fruit of the earth, being patient about it, until it receives the early and the late rains. You also, be patient. Establish your hearts, for the coming of the Lord is at hand" (James 5:7–8).

➤ Turn Your Sights on Him: This doesn't mean to do nothing. If you need a job, you still must look for employment and fill out applications. But pray that God opens the right doors for you and leads you down the right path. Ask Him to give you direction to make the right decisions for your future.

> ➤ Focus on God: While you wait, find ways to honor God and show compassion to others while you wait for His leading. You may consider volunteering at a homeless shelter or a soup kitchen. This will not only give you an opportunity to show God's love, but it will help you appreciate what you have, and you will be "strengthened with all power, according to his glorious might, for all endurance and patience with joy" (Colossians 1:11).

When "Bear" Bryant was on the team, he didn't know what was in store down the road for him and the Alabama faithful. He was not aware he would lead the Crimson Tide to such extraordinary heights. He played his role and was patient, and he later established a huge legacy. Bryant was not yet ready to coach the team, but he played the game and gained valuable experience that would lead to his later success.

Spiritually, you must wait on God's plan and allow Him to mature you for the right moment. His plans for us are much better than our own. Trust Him to write your story.

DAY 5
OVERCOME THE ODDS

January 1, 1942: Alabama 29, Texas A&M 21

The LORD is thy keeper: the LORD is thy shade upon thy right hand. —Psalm 121:5 KJV

Alabama finished the 1941 regular season with two losses. Although most teams would be satisfied with a record of 8–2, Coach Frank Thomas was not pleased.

He knew the Tide was better, but the losses to Vanderbilt and Mississippi State were on the books.

Nothing could change the past.

The team went on to the Cotton Bowl in Dallas, Texas, to face off against Texas A&M, which basically held a home-field advantage in the Lone Star State.

In the past, the Crimson Tide had entered bowl games with an undefeated record. Not this time. This was new territory, and Alabama blazed into Texas with a chip on its shoulder.

For the first time, they played the role of the underdog. *The Associated Press* ranked Bama at number twenty, while the Aggies were ninth in the nation.

Statistically, the Aggies dominated the game. Perhaps the most incredible game statistic was that Alabama had only one first down compared to thirteen for Texas A&M. One.

On the ground, the Aggies produced 115 yards while the Tide could only manage 59 yards rushing. The passing was no different. Bama only had 16 yards receiving while Texas piled up 194 yards in the air.

How in the world did Alabama win?

The defense rose to the occasion and picked off seven passes, which led to the victory.

After marching to a 29–7 lead, Coach Thomas put in his third string players, allowing the Aggie offense to score and make the game closer than the score portrayed.

Alabama used the fact that Texas A&M was predicted to win the game to fuel their fire. They overcame the obstacles and claimed the Cotton Bowl title.

Have you found yourself in a similar situation in life? Did you overcome or did you give in to defeat?

> We are troubled on every side, yet not distressed;
> we are perplexed, but not in despair; persecuted,
> but not forsaken; cast down, but not destroyed.
> —2 Corinthians 4:8–9 KJV

FAITH AND PRIDE

Have the odds been stacked against you before? Perhaps you have been laid off from work, the job market is scarce, and bills are due. Maybe you are faced with an illness that has turned your world upside down. Relationship struggles can also leave you emotionally exhausted and can invite discouragement and hopelessness. Why even play the game, right? Had Alabama entertained that notion, they would not have won the Cotton Bowl.

AND ROLL TIDE

Life's blitzes can leave you feeling as though you are on a third down with thirty-five yards to go. A score might seem impossible to pull off, but you have to huddle up and call the play. Rely on your linemen to block, and look for the open receiver downfield. He's there. You just have to make the pass. Here are some tips on how to pull off the big play and defy the odds:

➤ Focus on God's Mighty Power Instead of Your Problem: We have all been overwhelmed by challenges in life. However I'm always amazed at how the Lord delivers right on time. I shouldn't be, but I still marvel at His perfect timing. If you are able to set your sights on His promises to take care of you and truly accept that your needs will be supplied, you have made it over the first hurdle.

➤ Trust His Plan: There may have been many times when the play called in the huddle made you scratch your head and wonder how it was going to be successful. But the more you focus on the fact that God loves you and wants the best for you, the more you can put your trust in Him. "What time I am afraid, I will trust in thee" (Psalm 56:3 KJV).

➤ Surround Yourself with Likeminded Believers: You can gain strength when you talk with people in your church about your problems. Choose these people wisely, and make sure they will keep your confidence and commit to share your burden and pray for you. Join forces with your Christian brothers and sisters and seek God's guidance.

- ➢ Praise: No matter the situation, it is easier to bear when you worship the Lord. Your problems may not disappear, but they will be easier to handle knowing the Master is in charge. Praise God in anticipation, expecting great things as you trust Him to answer your prayers. "O give thanks unto the LORD; for he is good; for his mercy endureth for ever" (1 Chronicles 16:34 KJV).

- ➢ Anticipate the Blessings: Just like the Crimson Tide, you might face a big challenge where some people may not expect you to rise to the occasion. When you focus on the blessings of life instead of the negative, you will be poised to accept what God has in store for you. His answer may not always be what you want, but it will be what is best for you according to His plan. Trust the Master to give you the big victory you need. "For the LORD your God is he that goeth with you, to fight for you against your enemies, to save you" (Deuteronomy 20:4 KJV).

On paper, Alabama did not deserve to win the game. But contests are not always won with statistics. Victory comes to the one who is prepared and disciplined for battle. Put aside the naysayers and pessimists, and let the Lord be your lead blocker. Drop back in the pocket and release the perfect spiral to the receiver ready to score the go-ahead touchdown. Overcome the obstacles and claim your Cotton Bowl title in the end.

DAY 6
BE HUMBLE AND NOT OVERCONFIDENT

January 1, 1946: Alabama 34, USC 14

Do nothing from selfish ambition or conceit, but in humility count others more significant than yourselves.
—Philippians 2:3

The Alabama football team posted another undefeated season. They went 9–0 and romped over every opponent.

The closest game of the year was a 28–14 win over Georgia. The Crimson Tide had outscored the other teams by a total of 430–80.

The squad was a well-oiled machine and earned its sixth invitation to play in the prestigious Rose Bowl where they would match up against the University of Southern California, which basically enjoyed the home-field advantage in Pasadena.

More than 93,000 people attended the contest to watch the mighty Trojans take on the Tide.

USC head coach Jeff Cravath had overhauled the offense and shifted to a "T" formation, which allowed for several running backs to handle the ball.

Although the Trojans had won eight consecutive Rose Bowls, they struggled in the 1945 season to compile a 7–3 record. Still, the team wanted to face Alabama and prove it was in a better class of football programs.

After all, USC belonged in the Pacific Coast Conference (PCC) and looked down on the Southeastern Conference (SEC).

The Trojans started off on a bad note when they fumbled on the game's second play from scrimmage on their own fifteen-yard line. Five Alabama plays later, quarterback Hal Self dove into the end zone.

The second quarter saw touchdowns by Self and Lowell Tew, and the Tide was beginning to roll with a 20–0 halftime lead.

The second successful drive of the half was the result of a sixty-four-yard drive that took only four plays.

The third period was the same—Bama domination.

Alabama took the pigskin away from USC again, this time on the Trojan thirty-nine-yard line. Seven plays later, Norwood Hodges plunged into the end zone from one yard out for the 27–0 lead.

Crimson Tide quarterback Harry Gilmer connected on a twenty-yard pass to Self for the score to start the fourth quarter. A 34–0 lead prompted Coach Thomas to pull his starters and use the second string.

When it was over, Alabama outgained the mighty Trojans 351 yards to their 41. The men of Troy were stifled by the Bama defense to only six yards on the ground.

Gilmer was named MVP as he collected 113 yards on 16 carries.

Going into the game, the Trojans were confident and had something to prove. The biggest lesson they learned that day was to be careful what you ask for because you might just get it.

Day 6: Be Humble and Not Overconfident

Are you humble? What have events in your life taught you about humility?

> When pride comes, then comes disgrace, but with the humble is wisdom. —Proverbs 11:2

FAITH AND PRIDE

There is a difference between being confident and being arrogant. Do you sometimes feel as though you are ten-feet tall and bulletproof? Maybe you have a primo job and drive the best vehicle money can buy. There is nothing wrong with success, but if you like to flaunt, brag, and promote yourself, then you may need to revisit your motives.

AND ROLL TIDE

Humility is not a sign of weakness; it drives you to put your own needs aside and focus on others. It means you attend your child's school event rather than spend time with your buddies on the links. It means you take your wife to dinner after a long day at the office to shower your attention on her. It means you visit a friend who is sick, instead of shopping for your own pleasure. Priorities shift when you have important responsibilities. Here are some ways to make sure you stay humble:

➢ Confess Your Sins to God Each Day: Everyone has sinned and fallen short of God's glory (Romans 3:23). When you realize you are not perfect and need the Lord's help to make it through each day, this is a sign of humility. Take a few moments each morning to examine yourself and make sure your priorities line up with the Word of God.

➤ Submit to Authority: Today's culture promotes self and individualism. Social media is all about you and me and what we've done in the past two hours. The mantra out there is to take care of yourself first. That's why it can be difficult to recognize authority. Society has taken a negative view of police officers and other public servants. But peace can only come with respect for law and order. Show honor to those who are in charge, whether in public or in your own home. If you are married, it's a joint venture. If you are at home in your parents' house, obey their rules. "Servants, be subject to your masters with all respect, not only to the good and gentle but also to the unjust" (1 Peter 2:18).

➤ Accept Feedback: Don't let your ego interfere with your growth as a Christian. College football players must have confidence in their abilities and play hard. But if a player does something wrong, the coach will tell him. The same is true for you. Be willing to accept constructive criticism and instruction. No one likes to be told what they did wrong, but in the long run, it will make you a better person. Take a step back and learn from the feedback you receive.

➤ Serve Others: There is no better way to show submission and compassion than to help others. You can volunteer on a regular basis for a charity that promotes a cause special to your heart, or you could become involved in local government. No matter what you do, make sure you put the needs of other people before your own.

Day 6: Be Humble and Not Overconfident

➤ Forgive: This is perhaps the hardest yet the best way to be humble. When you forgive, you start anew, and it is possibly the greatest acts of humility you can do. Forgiveness is denial of self. "Whoever conceals his transgressions will not prosper, but he who confesses and forsakes them will obtain mercy" (Proverbs 28:13).

The Trojans were prideful before the game. Perhaps if they had shown humility prior to the contest and taken their competitors more seriously, Alabama may not have handed them such a bruising defeat. The Tide was going to roll anyway but had an additional incentive to teach a little lesson in humility to USC.

DAY 7
REKINDLE THE RELATIONSHIP

December 4, 1948: Alabama 55, Auburn 0

Draw near to God and He will draw near to you.
Cleanse your hands, you sinners; and purify your
hearts, you double-minded. —James 4:8 NKJV

The two teams had not met in forty-one years.

The last time Alabama played Auburn was in 1907, and that
game ended in a 6–6 tie.

The schools had previously faced off on a regular basis from
1893 up through 1907. But in 1908, due to trivial disputes, the
series was stopped.

The disagreements centered around how much per diem
players received and how many players each school should
bring to the rivalry.

Then there were the fans who argued about how much
better their team was. Of course, Alabama fans were always
right.

But the two universities finally got together, settled their
differences, and agreed to play the Iron Bowl once again. After
all, the drive from one to the other is only about three hours.

Alabama took a quick 7–0 in the first quarter when Gordon
Pettus connected with Butch Avinger for an eight-yard touchdown pass. Clem Welsh scored two touchdowns before the half
ended, and the lead was 21–0.

Ed Salem scored on a seventeen-yard run and later connected with Rebel Steiner for a fifty-three-yard scoring pass.

When it was over, the Tide had rolled to deliver a 55–0 thumping to Auburn.

The rivalry between the two schools is like none other in sports. When each game is completed, the talk for the next season begins immediately. Fans from both teams live for this game.

And, to think, for several years this routine showdown did not exist because of petty issues. What about you? Have you lost touch with people who used to be your friends? Maybe a falling out has separated you from a family member. Have you ever tried to make amends and restart the friendly rivalry?

> Therefore if there is any consolation in Christ, if any comfort of love, if any fellowship of the Spirit, if any affection and mercy, fulfill my joy by being like-minded, having the same love, being of one accord, of one mind.
> —Philippians 2:1–2 NKJV

FAITH AND PRIDE

Many things can lead to the separation of friendships. People grow apart. Jobs lead people in different directions, and new friends and priorities can form a wedge. Perhaps you fall into this scenario. Maybe you have a family member whose wrong decisions drove him away and out of touch. Or maybe years of mental or physical abuse led you to make a decision to break away from those you loved. Have you been hurt by someone close to you and vowed never to speak to them again? Did you cut off relations with your parents years ago, and there is something you have never forgiven them for?

AND ROLL TIDE

Maybe you've begun to think about the relationships you once had and decided to rekindle the bonds. Restoration is possible. People can change, especially if Christ is in their lives. Broken relationships can be repaired. Here are some tips to consider when you want to reconnect and rebuild these bonds:

➤ Make Sure All Parties Are on the Same Page: If you feel compelled to reestablish a lost relationship and reach out to someone, make sure to find out if they want it too. A mutual commitment is the first step to restoring a friendship. Don't force the issue.

➤ Be Humble: No matter who was at fault for the break-up or the distance between you, show humility and admit any wrongs. Don't assume responsibility for actions that were not yours, but if you are responsible, own up to it and admit it. "So do this, my son, and deliver yourself; for you have come into the hand of your friend: go and humble yourself; plead with your friend" (Proverbs 6:3 NKJV).

➤ Take Your Time: Relationships need to be cultivated. There is a time to plant, fertilize, and water. Don't rush a result just because you want it to happen overnight. Take the necessary steps and take it slow. Alabama and Auburn waited forty-one years to play again. Your situation hopefully will not take quite that long to heal, but it also may take more than a few days. Reach out and plant the seed.

➤ Seek Forgiveness: Remorse is just as important as humility. Admit if you were wrong, and if the other person was at fault, let it go and move forward. You can either choose to remember or choose to start over, but forgiveness will bring healing even if the other person does not apologize. "I even I, am He who blots out your transgressions for My own sake; and I will not remember your sins" (Isaiah 43:25 NKJV).

➤ Enjoy the Moment: When the relationship is restored, cherish each moment with that person. Things might never be the same again, or they might be better than before. Be happy, and never take the relationship for granted again.

Officials with Alabama and Auburn decided the time was right to rekindle their rivalry. They put aside their differences and met on common ground. The resurrection of one of the biggest rivalries in college sports provided a thrill for the fans from both universities that continues today. But it took someone to get the ball rolling. Pride was put aside, and a decision was made for the best of all parties involved.

DAY 8
GIVE IT UP

January 1, 1962: Alabama 10, Arkansas 3

May the God of hope fill you with all joy and peace in believing, so that by the power of the Holy Spirit you may abound in hope. —Romans 15:13

Bear Bryant was in his first national championship game as a coach. He guided the number-one ranked Tide to a perfect 10–0 season.

The Alabama defense gave up twenty-two points all season while the offense blistered opponents with 287. In the final five regular season games, no team scored on the Crimson Tide.

Bryant's team wasted little time and scored in six plays to grab a 7–0 lead at Tulane Stadium in New Orleans, Louisiana.

Quarterback Pat Trammell faked out the Razorback defense and pretended to pass, then he tucked the ball and scampered into the end zone from twelve yards out.

During the second half, Alabama's Butch Wilson picked off a pass from Arkansas quarterback George McKinney and returned it to the twenty-yard line in the red zone.

That set up a field goal from Tim Davis to boost the lead to 10–0 at the break.

Arkansas had a chance to cut the deficit before halftime but missed a chip-shot field goal.

The Razorbacks had two more chances to cut into the lead in the third quarter. One field goal attempt was blocked while the second went through the uprights to bring the team within a touchdown of Alabama.

The three points was the first score on the Tide defense in five games.

With a few minutes left to play, McKinney rallied the troops and orchestrated a drive that ended when Wilson picked off his second pass to end the game and secure the Tide's Sugar Bowl and National Championship title.

After the game, both teams wanted the game ball, but Bryant was said to have told his players to let Arkansas have the pigskin.

In the end, it was the only thing Alabama gave up to Arkansas all day.

What can you relinquish? Will you surrender your bad habits?

> For you know that the testing of your faith produces steadfastness. —James 1:3

FAITH AND PRIDE

We all have habits or things we could and should give up for our faith to grow. Bad habits also can damage your reputation among potential Christians who might look to you as a role model. For example, you might think twice about hanging out in nightclubs while proclaiming your allegiance to the Lord. The Bible instructs us to abstain from the appearance of evil. You can have fun, but you could pick more family-friendly locations to enjoy yourself with your friends. Perhaps you need to adjust your language when you become angry or upset. Foul words can also hinder your witness to others.

Day 8: Give It Up

AND ROLL TIDE

You might have personal convictions that you need to work on and activities you need to give up to better enjoy the blessings of the Lord. If He convicts you of an act, then listen and obey. Here are some habits you might not think of that you need to toss in the garbage can.

> The World: The world offers glamour and fame but will turn its back on you faster than Alabama scored in the opening quarter of the Sugar Bowl. It will compete for your love and affection and will place distractions in your way between you and God. Set yourself apart and be a witness of God's saving power. Give it up.

> Worrying: To worry about something out of your control is normal and a complete waste of time. It's also dangerous. Jesus told His disciples a handful of times in Luke 12 not to worry. You cannot undo the past or control your destiny. Place both in God's hands and move on. This doesn't mean you just stand idle and don't do anything. But it suggests that you let the Lord take over and solve your problems. John Wayne's character, Rooster Cogburn, said in the film *True Grit*, "Looking back is a bad habit." Look ahead and anticipate the good things God has in store for you. "Casting all your anxieties on him, because he cares for you" (1 Peter 5:7). Give it up.

> The Wrong Crowd: In the Book of Proverbs, you are instructed to choose your friends wisely. (See Proverbs 13:20; 14:6–7; 22:24–25.) If you hang out with friends who are like-minded, they can help build and strengthen your faith. But distance yourself from people who are

negative and discourage you from serving the Lord. Also beware of those in the church who gossip and criticize others. Give it up.

➤ Self: You could be the biggest hindrance to your own faith and not even be aware. Success and happiness are all good, but don't let them go to your head. Your faith can be strengthened by volunteering your time to worthy and just causes. Get yourself and your own needs out of the way and help others. "To put off your old self, which belongs to your former manner of life and is corrupt through deceitful desires, and to be renewed in the spirit of your minds, and to put on the new self, created after the likeness of God in true righteousness and holiness" (Ephesians 4:22–24). Give it up.

➤ Bitterness: There is no place in a Christian's life for bitterness that can eat at you and rob you of joy and happiness. When you hold a grudge against someone, it can ruin your relationship and make you mean and hateful. "Let all bitterness and wrath and anger and clamor and slander be put away from you, along with all malice" (v. 31). Give it up.

Coach Bear Bryant let Arkansas have the ball. He gave it up. What he took back with him was the Sugar Bowl trophy and title of National Champion. He didn't need the pigskin. Alabama earned the win and enjoyed the sweet taste of victory. Give up your bad habits, and you can do the same.

DAY 9
SHARE YOUR TESTIMONY

January 1, 1966: Alabama 39, Nebraska 28

Howbeit Jesus suffered him not, but saith unto him, go home to thy friends, and tell them how great things the Lord hath done for thee, and hath had compassion on thee. —Mark 5:19 KJV

The stage was set. Everyone knew what to expect now.

Number-one ranked Michigan State lost in the Rose Bowl, and number-two Arkansas was defeated in the Cotton Bowl earlier in the day.

Alabama, ranked fourth by *The Associated Press*, had a legitimate chance to win a National Championship before the day was over. But Nebraska, ranked third, was in the way.

The Crimson Tide, under the direction of Coach Bear Bryant, posted a regular season record of 8–1–1. A one-point loss to Georgia on opening weekend and a tie with Tennessee were the team's only blemishes.

But new life had been breathed into them. The game mattered more now than ever.

Alabama scored on a thirty-two-yard touchdown pass from Steve Sloan to Ray Perkins to take a 7–0 lead.

Nebraska countered when quarterback Bob Churchich found Tony Jeter for a thirty-three-yard scoring pass.

The Tide rolled back and scored on a four-yard run by Les Kelly and again claimed the lead 14—7, increasing their advantage to 24—7 at the half thanks to another Slone-Perkins combination for a score and a field goal.

The Cornhuskers answered to begin the third quarter when Churchich found Ben Gregory for a forty-nine-yard touchdown.

The game was like a heavyweight-boxing match as both teams countered on the scoreboard.

Alabama's Steve Bowman plunged into the end zone from one yard out for a 32—13 lead. Then Churchich responded and dove in from a yard out to narrow the gap 32—20.

Bowman increased the Bama lead to 39—20 after he scampered in from three yards out.

Once again, Nebraska came back and scored when Churchich found Jeter on a fourteen-yard touchdown pass.

But that was as close as the score would get, and Alabama knocked off Nebraska to win the Orange Bowl.

After the game, *The Associated Press* put Alabama at the number-one spot and awarded them the 1965 National Championship. The choice was obvious.

However, some other selectors for the title, including the UPI (United Press International), recognized Michigan State along with Alabama as National Champions.

But the final AP Poll is what mattered, and it listed the Tide at the top.

Alabama won the title outright and did not wish to share it with anyone.

But as Christians, there is something we are expected to share—our testimony. Others need to hear it, and telling your redemption story will put you at the top of your game.

Give thanks unto the LORD, call upon his name, make known his deeds among the people. —1 Chronicles 16:8 KJV

FAITH AND PRIDE

Do you like to share your faith with others? Are you hesitant at times to tell friends about the Lord and His grace? Do you feel uncomfortable taking a stand when you are with a group of nonbelievers? This can be intimidating, but ask God for courage to stand against the devil as he encourages you to hold your tongue. People who are unsaved need to hear the gospel—and they also need to see it in you.

AND ROLL TIDE

When you have a wonderful experience in life, most of the time you will tell everyone you know via social media, and you can't wait to share the exciting news. If your son hits a homerun, you immediately post it on Facebook. You are quick to post photos of your daughter with her winning science-fair trophy. You are proud, and that's great. But you should take the same approach to your Christian testimony. You don't need to be brash or condemning, but you need to let your light shine. Here are some reasons why:

> ➤ You Story Is Unique: Your experience is owned by you alone. If you overcame a tragedy in life or if you were raised in church to know right from wrong, your story is one-of-a-kind. It doesn't have to be earthshattering, but it is amazing. There was a time when you realized you

needed a Savior, and He came to your rescue. Tell others about it with a smile.

➢ God Tells Us to Share: This is cut and dry. You cannot argue this point. "But sanctify the Lord God in your hearts: and be ready always to give an answer to every man that asketh you a reason of the hope that is in you with meekness and fear" (1 Peter 3:15 KJV).

➢ Sharing Your Testimony Emboldens You and Gives You Courage: Practice makes perfect. The more you share your testimony with others, the more comfortable you feel, and it becomes part of your personal identity.

➢ You Inspire Others: You never know what people are searching for in the world. What you say to someone about God's grace might be what they needed to hear at that exact moment. People love to hear an inspirational message, and it might encourage someone in need to search for the Savior just like you did.

➢ Your Testimony Glorifies the Lord: This is the best reason. Your testimony magnifies and praises God for His goodness to you. When you describe your story, make sure you tell everyone who listens about how your life changed for the better. Don't dwell on your past; rather make a point to tell everyone how you needed your life to go in the right direction. Make sure they know it can happen for them too. A testimony should be positive, heartfelt, and genuine. Most of all, it should lift up the name of the Lord. "Let the redeemed of the LORD say so, whom he hath redeemed from the hand of the enemy" (Psalm 107:2 KJV).

Day 9: Share Your Testimony

Many college football enthusiasts recognize that Alabama won the national title in 1965. But you might receive another opinion from Michigan State fans. Nonetheless, the AP deemed the Tide as the best that year. And they are not willing to share the crown, and with just reason. You, on other hand, have no excuse to keep the goodness of God's love to yourself. Share it.

DAY 10
STAY OUT OF THE MUD

December 2, 1967: Alabama 7, Auburn 3

No temptation has overtaken you that is not common to man. God is faithful, and he will not let you be tempted beyond your ability, but with the temptation he will also provide the way of escape, that you may be able to endure it. —1 Corinthians 10:13

There is nothing like the Iron Bowl. For many Alabama fans, it means more than the National Championship—well maybe not, but it's close.

The Tide rolled into the game at Legion Field ranked number eight with a record of 7–1–1 while Auburn was 6–3. A heavy downpour of rain made the field a muddy mess.

The Tigers had three chances to score in the first half, but the stubborn Bama defense made two goal-line stands. The game was scoreless at the break.

Auburn's defense forced a muffed punt by Alabama, and the Tigers took over inside the Tide's forty-yard line. They settled for a thirty-seven-yard field goal and took a 3–0 lead in the third quarter.

Both teams struggled to find footing, and offensive production was difficult. But Alabama quarterback Ken Stabler adjusted and came through for the Tide in a big way.

From his own forty-seven-yard line, he ran an option play and kept the ball. The lanky signal caller picked his way through the defense and the slop. He rumbled the distance, outran the defenders, and crossed the goal line for the touchdown and the go-ahead score for the 7–3 win.

The play is forever known as the "run in the mud."

Have you had to push through some difficult challenges? What struggles have taken you through the mud?

> Do not be conformed to this world, but be transformed by the renewal of your mind, that by testing you may discern what is the will of God, what is good and acceptable and perfect. —Romans 12:2

FAITH AND PRIDE

Has Satan chased you through the mud and storms of life? Were you able to outrun the defense and score the winning touchdown? There are many muddy obstacles that can try to tackle you for a loss and stop you from reaching the goal of serving the Lord. You might be tormented by your past or face situations that tempt you. You might be in recovery from addiction or heading toward a relationship crisis. The devil does not want you to win the game, and he will use the mud to slow you down.

AND ROLL TIDE

Ken Stabler had to use his blockers and take short and choppy steps to get through the mud. He could not run the way he normally would, so he had to adjust to the conditions and keep his eye on the goal. He made it through in less-than-desirable conditions. You can too. Just because you have fallen in the slop does not mean you have to stay there. There is a goal line in sight. Here are some tips to manage your way through the muck and mire of life:

Day 10: Stay Out of the Mud

➤ Know Your Weakness: Shortcomings can be tough to admit, but once you identify the source of the mud and get rid of it, the stronger you will become. Not everyone is tempted in the same way. Some might be drawn to prescription pain medicine while others might struggle with gambling or alcohol. One weakness might be the flesh and your eyes may wander while another might be gossip and a rumoring tongue. Challenge Satan and whatever he uses to hold you down. "But each person is tempted when he is lured and enticed by his own desire. Then desire when it has conceived gives birth to sin, and sin when it is fully grown brings forth death" (James 1:14–15).

➤ Run from the Temptation: The devil tries to entice you in the areas where you are most weak and vulnerable. Be smart, and stay away from environments where you are exposed to the things you have the most trouble giving in to. For example, if you struggle with alcohol, don't go to a bar. Recognize those circumstances that can lure you into sin, and distance yourself from threats as much as possible. Ken Stabler ran from the defenders. He did not run to them because they would have stopped him from getting to the end zone. You need to do the same. Run away and stay out of the mud. "And lead us not into temptation, but deliver us from evil" (Matthew 6:13).

➤ Find Strength in the Word: Find verses that give you encouragement, and memorize them to help you in times of struggle. This is a wonderful defense mechanism that can fend off the devil's attacks. "For the word of God is living and active, sharper than any two-edged sword" (Hebrews 4:12).

➤ Don't Give Up: Never be complacent about temptation or sin in your life. You will mess up, but you must learn from your actions and vow to not repeat them. Don't beat yourself up, but take on responsibility. Realize that you are human and will have battles with temptation, but you must not quit. You have choices to make, and you need to let God help you. Allow Him to pull you out of the mud pit, spray you off, and shine you up to be a light for Him.

➤ Find Christian Friends to Rally around You: Form an accountability group and support each other. This can be a small gathering of people who will hold your feet to the fire. You can discuss life's struggles and victories during the times you share together. Find people who will be honest with you and call you out if you make a mistake. "Iron sharpens iron, and one man sharpens another" (Proverbs 27:17).

Ken Stabler did not make a direct path to the end zone through the mud. He zigzagged his way back and forth to avoid the tacklers. You have to do the same thing in life. Recognize who you are up against, and run away from them. Let the Lord block for you and escort you to the end zone for the score.

DAY 11
TAKE ON THE BLITZ

October 4, 1969: Alabama 33, Ole Miss 32

Now I urge you, brethren, note those who cause divisions and offenses, contrary to the doctrine which you learned, and avoid them. —Roman 16:17 NKJV

The game was the first one to be broadcast on national television in prime time.

Legion Field in Birmingham, Alabama, played host to number-fifteen Crimson Tide and the Ole Miss Rebels, who entered ranked twentieth by *The Associated Press*.

The offensive shootout set nine SEC records and one NCAA record at the time.

Both teams were tied 7–7 at the end of the first quarter, thanks to a Johnny Musso one-yard plunge for Alabama followed by a two-yard scamper by Ole Miss quarterback Archie Manning.

Bubba Sawyer gave the Tide a 14–7 lead at the break after he went seventeen yards with the ball into the end zone.

The Rebels answered in the third quarter when Manning found Floyd Franks for an eleven-yard touchdown.

Alabama quickly responded when Musso crossed from one yard out. Manning followed for Ole Miss with a seventeen-yard touchdown dash. At the end of the third quarter, Alabama led 21–20.

Manning kept the Rebels in the game when he fired a two-yard scoring pass to Riley Myers and added a one-yard touchdown run.

Alabama got a touchdown from quarterback Scott Hunter to bring the Tide to within five points at 32–27.

The stage was set for a dramatic comeback.

The Tide faced a fourth-down and goal from the Rebel fourteen-yard line when a time out was called.

There was some confusion on the sideline, and Hunter asked Coach Bear Bryant what to run. With time slipping before the next play, Bryant barked out his instructions to run the best play they had.

Hunter called out, "Fire Red Right, Max Protect 56 Comeback," because he anticipated a blitz from the defense. He was right. The ball was snapped, and the linebackers bolted for him.

Musso stepped up and took on the blocker, who would have sacked Hunter for the loss. But the block allowed Hunter to find George Ranager in the end zone for the game-winning catch.

Hunter turned in a magnificent performance and completed twenty-two of twenty-nine passes for three hundred yards in perhaps his finest game.

But if it had not been for Musso's block, defeat would have been eminent. He was able to avoid the rush and fire the pass to win the game.

> For those who are such do not serve our Lord Jesus Christ, but their own belly, and by smooth words and flattering speech deceive the hearts of the simple. — Romans 16:18 NKJV

FAITH AND PRIDE

The forces of evil want nothing more than to tackle you for a loss and cause you to lose the game. They have devised a scheme that involves an all-out blitz for your soul. They are clever and won't give away the game plan. Instead they use subtle tactics to wear you down, and their strategy is to penetrate your heart and mind until you give up and turn your back on your team.

AND ROLL TIDE

When Scott Hunter called out the play that won the game, he was prepared mentally because the team practiced every day. He anticipated the defense to come after him and knew Johnny Musso could handle the assignment. The same is true for you as a believer. You must recognize when the devil is about to tackle you. Here is his game plan and the tools he might use:

> ➢ Division: If Satan can drive a wedge between you and your family, friends, or the church, he has a chance to win. He will not play fair and will resort to lies to fuel the fire. You must be able to see through this and stay united with your loved ones. "Behold, how good and how pleasant it is for brethren to dwell together in unity!" (Psalm 133:1 NKJV).

> ➢ Discouragement: If you are rejected or make a huge mistake, you might feel unworthy and entertain feelings of giving up on your journey. Fight back with a positive attitude, and hold daily devotions that will give you strength. If you need to seek personal help, talk to your pastor or friends about how you feel.

> Immorality: The devil will try to lead you into compromising positions. This maneuver is easier now with social media, and he will use it to try to persuade you to communicate with someone you should not be in touch with. He can arrange chance encounters at work that might lead to the breakup of the home. You need to be proactive and see this defensive alignment and make sure your offensive line is up to the task.

> Arrogance: Don't think that these things can't happen to you. You must put on the armor of God to fight against Satan's trap. When you think you don't need to read your Bible, attend church, and pray, then you are taking a dangerous risk. Show devotion to the Lord and spend as much time with Him and your fellow believers as possible. "Therefore humble yourselves under the mighty hand of God, that He may exalt you in due time" (1 Peter 5:6 NKJV).

> Hate and Jealousy: Satan will use feelings of hate and jealousy to strengthen his grip on you, if you allow him to break through the line. If someone is promoted in front of you or gets all the attention you believe you are entitled to, those emotions can cross the neutral zone. If someone doesn't repay you or takes you for granted, you might grow bitter. Kick this attempt to tackle you over the goal post for the extra point. Love others and be happy when good things happen to them. "And walk in love, as Christ also has loved us and given Himself for us, an offering and a sacrifice to God for a sweet-smelling aroma" (Ephesians 5:2 NKJV).

Day 11: Take On the Blitz

Hunter called the right play, and everyone did their part. The pass was executed, and Bama won the close game for the nation to see. When you recognize the blitz of the defense, step up and block the linebackers in your life to win a prime-time victory.

DAY 12
PUNT BAMA PUNT

December 2, 1972: Auburn 17, Alabama 16

If we confess our sins, he is faithful and just to forgive
us our sins, and to cleanse us from all unrighteousness.
—1 John 1:9 KJV

Undefeated and second-ranked Alabama (10–0) hosted Auburn
(8–1) at Legion Field in Birmingham and had control of the
game.

The Tide entered the game favored by two touchdowns and
took a commanding 16–0 lead with ten minutes to play in the
game. The game was in the bag.

Auburn managed to get on the board with a field goal to
cut the lead 16–3.

On the next drive, Alabama was forced to punt from its
own territory. All the Tide had to do was boot the ball to the
other side of the field and force Auburn to burn time and go
the length.

Instead, Bill Newton burst through the line and blocked
the punt for Auburn. David Langer scooped up the ball and ran
it twenty-five yards for the touchdown and, just like that, the
game was 16–10.

Alabama got the ball back and was forced to punt once
again.

The chances of another block were slim, and Coach Bear Bryant felt comfortable that his special teams would be successful this time.

But déjà vu happened, and Newton once again blocked the punt, and Langer returned it for a touchdown.

Boom. Auburn led 17–16.

What are the odds of the same player blocking two punts and the same other player returning the ball for touchdowns on two consecutive possessions?

Alabama got the pigskin back and had a chance to make a final drive to get into scoring position, but Langer intercepted a pass and stopped the comeback.

Twice the offensive line let the defense through, and the result was terrible for the Tide.

To permit a player to block a punt once was a mistake. But to allow it to happen two times in a row was a complete breakdown.

Bama did not properly defend the line and consequently lost the game.

> And when ye stand praying, forgive, if ye have ought against any: that your Father also which is in heaven may forgive you your trespass. —Mark 11:25 KJV

What do you do when the devil comes at you from all sides? Do you allow him to find your weakness and continue to break through to block your punts? Will your mistakes continue to leave a crease in the line for the forces of evil to break through?

FAITH AND PRIDE

When you make a mistake, the devil will pound at you and try to get you to repeat your slipup over and again. He will tell you that you cannot live the Christian life. He will lie to you and remind you that your past mishaps will come back to haunt you. He will whisper in your ear that you are unforgivable and worthless. He wants to penetrate your line of defense and block your punt as many times as he can. His goal is to demoralize you and crush your spirits. His plan is to destroy you and capture your soul. He is ruthless.

AND ROLL TIDE

Many football teams will scout the opposition the week prior to the matchup and watch game films to try to pinpoint the weaknesses of their opponents. Auburn's research obviously led to two outstanding plays that secured the big win. Their rush to block the punt was calculated and executed to perfection. They used video from past Alabama games to find opportunities for victory. Does your past bother you? Does it creep up to the line and rush your kicker? The best line of defense is to forgive yourself. Here are some tips to help you kick the ball safely down the field:

> ➢ Acknowledge Your Mistake and Move On: There is no benefit that comes by looking over your shoulder with regret. That is a complete waste of time. The only thing that can be a result is education. Learn from it and move on. Once you recognize your mistake, repent and ask God to forgive you, and proceed forward.

- ➤ Remember You Are Not a Failure: Just because you have failed at one thing does not mean you fail in everything. Coach Bear Bryant did not view the loss in the Iron Bowl as a reason to give up. Instead, he learned from it and used the experience to better prepare his team for the next game. Keep fighting and stay positive.

- ➤ View Yourself as God's Child: You are a child of the King. Never worry about how others view you when you make a mistake. You are royalty, and His love for you is the only thing that matters. "Behold, what manner of love the Father hath bestowed upon us, that we should be called the sons of God" (1 John 3:1).

- ➤ Learn: The best way to prevent the act from taking place again is to review what went wrong and make the appropriate changes. Do you think Alabama ever had two punts blocked back-to-back ever again? Adjustments were made. Life is the best teacher, and you will learn from your failures. You will make more mistakes than victories, and failure does not have to be final.

- ➤ Forgive: Once you have followed the previous steps in this list, be ready to forgive yourself as well. If you don't, your mistakes will haunt you and follow you forever. You will be in bondage to them, and they will consume your life and thoughts. But when God forgives you, you forgive yourself, and the chains are broken and you are free. "Let us break their bands asunder, and cast away their cords from us" (Psalm 2:3 KJV).

Day 12: Punt Bama Punt

Alabama lost a heartbreaker to its rivals that taught them a lifelong lesson. Seal up the cracks in your life that the devil can penetrate. Form a strong offensive line that will help in situations when you feel you are outnumbered. Be sure to never let the forces of evil block the punt a second time in a row. Learn from your mistakes.

DAY 13
MAKE THE STAND

January 1, 1979: Alabama 14, Penn State 7

Preaching the kingdom of God, and teaching those things which concern the Lord Jesus Christ, with all confidence, no man forbidding him. —Acts 28:31 KJV

This game was the matchup everyone wanted.

Top-ranked Penn State (11–0) faced number-two Alabama for all the marbles. The Sugar Bowl in New Orleans would decide the National Championship.

The Nittany Lion's defense was rock solid, while the Crimson Tide boasted a powerful running game. One of them would have to step up its game to take home the title.

Neither team scored in the first quarter, and both squads tried to establish momentum and find a suitable attack.

With 1:32 left to play before halftime, the Tide started at its own twenty-yard line. Fullback Tony Nathan bolted for thirty yards for Alabama, and quarterback Jeff Rutledge later found Bruce Bolton in the end zone to give them a 7–0 lead at the break.

By the intermission, Alabama had set the stage and whipped off 214 total yards against the stingy Penn State defense.

The Nittany Lions struggled to find their offensive rhythm and was dropped to minus seven yards rushing and only twenty-nine yards in the air.

In the third period, the Penn State defense stiffened and picked off a Rutledge pass that was returned into Tide territory.

Quarterback Chuck Fusina found receiver Scott Fitzkee for a seventeen-yard touchdown pass, and the Nittany Lions tied the game 7–7.

Later in the third, Penn State punted, and Lou Ikner returned the ball sixty-two yards inside the red zone to the ten-yard line.

Alabama tailback Major Ogilvie then scampered in to retake the lead 14–7.

Penn State needed a big play, and it came at the right moment.

Ogilvie, who had just put the Tide on top, fumbled a pitch from Rutledge, and the Lions recovered deep in Alabama territory.

Penn State drove the ball inside the eight-yard line for first and goal.

Fitzkee caught a pass and was forced out of bounds inches away from the goal line.

Third and goal.

Fullback Matt Suhey tried to plow into the end zone but was met with force from Alabama's Curtis McGriff and Rich Wingo.

Fourth and goal.

Penn State was determined to run it in, but Mike Guman was stopped cold by Barry Krauss and Murray Legg with inches to go.

But the game wasn't over.

Alabama was forced to punt and shanked it from the end zone to their own thirty-yard line, but Penn State was called for having twelve players on the field, and the Tide kept the ball.

The Nittany Lions eventually got the ball back with just over a minute to play but could not muster up an effective comeback and failed to convert on a fourth-down pass.

Coach Bryant earned his fifth National Title, and the Tide was the team that showed a boldness at the line.

And for me, that utterance may be given unto me, that I may open my mouth boldly, to make known the mystery of the gospel. —Ephesians 6:19 KJV

FAITH AND PRIDE

Do you need a reason to stand strong in your faith? Have you been through a situation where you needed to make a stand for God? There are times when you need to be bold, stand firm, and not back down.

AND ROLL TIDE

Chances are, you won't find yourself in a goal-line stand on national television, but you can make an impact where you are. Here are some tips to be bold in your journey:

➢ Be Confident: The Tide had to believe in themselves as a team or they would have given up the score. Rely on the Lord to help you make your stand, and don't back down from the charging offense.

➢ Pray: Thank God publicly before you eat meals. You don't have to put on a show and draw attention to yourself. Just make it subtle and sincere. When people see you bow your head in prayer, they might be encouraged to do the same. "For there is one God, and one mediator between God and men, the man Christ Jesus" (1 Timothy 2:5 KJV).

➤ Use Social Media: Let your followers on social media know where you stand, but don't drive them away. Post an occasional sentence of inspiration with a Scripture passage attached. Add a line to your profile that tells everyone you love the Lord. For example, Tua Tagovailoa, a well-known Alabama quarterback, who has more than a quarter of a million followers on Twitter, puts Scripture on his profile page to expose his followers to the gospel. He makes it clear what's important to him. When your friends and followers know where you stand, you will become more accountable in your Christian journey. "And blessed be his glorious name for ever: and let the whole earth be filled with his glory; amen, and amen" (Psalm 72:19 KJV).

➤ Testify in Church: Telling your story will make you a stronger Christian. Just a few simple words of thanks will suffice. Your personal story can give others hope and will also let those around you know how grateful you are for God's mercy. "Be not thou therefore ashamed of the testimony of our Lord, nor of me his prisoner: but be thou partaker of the afflictions of the gospel according to the power of God" (2 Timothy 1:8 KJV).

➤ Lead a Bible Study: Gather a group of friends and open up your home for a time of devotion once a week or perhaps monthly. Use this time to share your personal testimony and encourage others to share their stories too. Present

Day 13: Make the Stand

the plan of salvation at each meeting, and give attendees an invitation to pray and ask Jesus into their hearts.

If you want to make a bold goal-line stand, try these methods. Express your love for the Lord on social media. Make it a point to testify in church and thank God for your blessings. Go deeper in the Word and pray for opportunities to lead others to Christ. You might just win the National Title.

DAY 14
GET BACK ON TOP

January 1, 1980: Alabama 24, Arkansas 9

"Return, O faithless sons; I will heal your faithlessness." "Behold, we come to you, for you are the LORD our God." —Jeremiah 3:22

The Crimson Tide entered the 1980 Sugar Bowl in New Orleans, Louisiana, undefeated and was poised to give legendary Coach Bear Bryant his first ever 12–0 season.

Alabama, which had been ranked first, slipped to number two on *The Associated Press* poll and faced number-six ranked Arkansas, who came in 10–1.

The game started off slow for Alabama when Don McNeal bobbled the opening kickoff and Arkansas took over at the twenty-five-yard line. The Hogs connected on a field goal for the early 3–0 lead.

With 6:37 left in the first period, Alabama's Major Ogilvie ran twenty-two yards for the score and capped an eighty-two-yard drive in seven plays for the 7–3 lead.

The Tide defense stepped up and forced a Razorback fumble on their own twenty-two-yard line. Ogilvie again scored a few plays later on a one-yard plunge for the 14–3 advantage. A field goal in the second quarter boosted the lead to 17–3 at the break.

Arkansas took the third quarter kickoff and answered with an eight-yard drive for a touchdown to cut the lead to 17–9.

The Crimson Tide offense countered with an impressive drive that covered ninety-eight yards in nine plays.

Steve Whitman plowed into the end zone from twelve yards out with 8:59 left in the game to boost the Bama lead to 24–9.

The numbers on both sides were even. Alabama outgained the Hogs 354 yards to 343.

On the ground, the Tide rolled for 284 yards while Arkansas passed for 245.

The win gave Bryant his sixth national championship and lifted Alabama back to the number-one spot on both the AP and United Press polls, right where it should have been all along.

Have you found yourself slipping in your Christian life and don't know why? Has something caused you to drift a little and fall in the rankings?

Why then has this people turned away in perpetual backsliding? They hold fast to deceit; they refuse to return. —Jeremiah 8:5

FAITH AND PRIDE

In today's hustle and bustle world with everyone's fast-paced lifestyles, you might easily become distracted and ignore your relationship with God by placing it on the backburner. This may not be your intention, but it can happen if you are not careful. You have a job that demands a lot of your time, the kids have ball games, and you have social events to attend. Life is busy. You might wake up one Sunday morning and roll over and tell the Lord you will go to His house next week. Then instead of reading your Bible, you flip on the SEC Network and watch football. You tell yourself you will get around to your prayers, but before you know it, the day has slipped away.

AND ROLL TIDE

The drift from the Lord's presence is a slow fade. It doesn't happen overnight. The devil will gradually pull you away until you find a way to justify your actions and stop focusing on your walk with Christ. But Alabama and Coach Bryant knew that it took dedication and practice to win the National Championship. If a player did not know his assignment, the coaches brought it to his attention and got it fixed. Take heed of all warning signs before you find yourself too far down in the score to come back. Here are a few to look for:

➢ Ignoring God's Word: Reading the Bible takes discipline and dedication. There may be portions you don't understand or don't like, but that's not a reason to abandon your obligation to read His game plan. Find a study Bible that helps to explain, or meet with your pastor for assistance. Ask God for wisdom, and allow His Word to feed your soul. "The one who rejects me and does not receive my words has a judge; the word that I have spoken will judge him on the last day" (John 12:48).

➢ Looking Back on Past Sin: This might happen if you have never sought forgiveness for past transgressions. Maybe there is a little piece of you that wants to keep a little piece of your past in your back pocket. This is not a good idea, and you need to repent and get your sins under the blood of Jesus and tossed into the sea of forgetfulness. Never look back.

➢ Neglecting Your Responsibilities: You have an obligation to lead your family by example and put God first. While it's great to possess a good work ethic and hold yourself to a high moral compass, make church attendance, prayer, and God's Word the main priorities in your home. When things of the world take precedence, they can draw you away from serving God the way you should.

➢ Hiding from Your Calling: You might be hearing the Lord calling you into a ministry or to do something you don't feel worthy to do. Sometimes people turn their back on God out of fear and anxiety. He will not call you to embarrass you or defeat your enthusiasm. The Lord might want you to give up a valuable possession or do something that will take you out of your comfort zone. Don't rebel—give in and say yes. "How shall we escape if we neglect such a great salvation? It was declared at first by the Lord, and it was attested to us by those who heard" (Hebrews 2:3).

➢ Disobeying the Lord: What would happen if Coach Bear Bryant told a player to do something and the player did not adhere to his instructions? No doubt, he would end up on the sidelines. God is the same way. When you say no, you inflict pain and suffering on yourself. Obey your Heavenly Father, and you will continue to be a part of the action. "Why do you call me 'Lord, Lord,' and not do what I tell you?" (Luke 6:46).

Day 14: Get Back on Top

We all become busy in life and need to slow down and return to the basics and the fundamentals of being a Christian. Watch out for the penalty flags and get back in the huddle and regroup. Recognize the defense, call the right play to win the game, and make sure to get back on top where you need to be for God.

DAY 15
LEARN AND MOVE ON

November 28, 1981: Alabama 28, Auburn 17

> He who covers his sins will not prosper, but
> whoever confesses and forsakes them will have
> mercy. —Proverbs 28:13 NKJV

A nifty shovel pass from Ken Coley to Jesse Bendross put
Alabama ahead 14–7 in the third quarter against rival Auburn
in the Iron bowl.

But there was a lot of football yet to be played.

The Tide's wide receiver, Joey Jones, had worked his way
into the lineup as a young sophomore and became the team's
main punt returner.

However, he muffed back-to-back kicks, which both
resulted in Auburn scores as the Tigers grabbed a 17–14 lead.

But the Tide rolled back when Walter Lewis connected
with Bendross for a thirty-eight-yard touchdown strike to take
the lead 21–14 with just over ten minutes to play.

With 7:07 remaining in the grudge match, Linnie Patrick
scampered fifteen yards into the end zone for Bama to put the
game out of reach at 28–17.

Although Jones made two critical mistakes that game, he
went on to enjoy a productive career and was an All-SEC pick
his senior season.

Mistakes will happen both on and off the field for a player. But character is built and established on how one responds to adversity and rises to the occasion to become a winner. Jones worked hard and made improvements on the field and enjoyed a solid career in Alabama.

The same applies to everyday life. People will mess up along the journey, but the way they deal with it will determine everything.

Have you lost your temper in front of others and said some things you regret? Have you tarnished your reputation by visiting a questionable establishment where you should not have been seen?

Did you ask God and those you offended to forgive you? Do you want to do better?

> Therefore humble yourselves under the mighty hand of God, that He may exalt you in due time. —1 Peter 5:6 NKJV

FAITH AND PRIDE

We have all been there. Once words leave the lips, it's too late to grab and put them back in your mouth before the damage is done. You might not intend to hurt a person, but an offensive word or comment can slip out quickly. Perhaps you did something that caused someone to question your salvation or you borrowed an item you never returned. Mistakes are common, but if left unaccounted for, they will negatively impact your Christian witness.

AND ROLL TIDE

When you recognize your mistakes and strive to make amends, you will be on the path to victory. Bounce back, and do your best to stay on a straight path to the championship. If you give up and expect yourself to mess up again, you will, and the mistakes will continue to become even more offensive. Sin will always take you further than you plan to go. Here are some things that can cause God's referees to call you off-sides:

➤ Refusing to Forgive: Maybe someone has hurt you or a loved one and you find it difficult to turn it over to God. Unforgiveness can fester and turn into bitterness and hate. You never intend for this to happen, but Satan uses your wounded emotions to set a trap for you to fail. If you find it difficult to forgive, talk to your pastor or confide in a professional. Ask God to give you peace about the situation and grant you the power to let it go. "Looking carefully lest anyone fall short of the grace of God; lest any root bitterness springing up cause trouble, and by this many become defiled" (Hebrews 12:15 NKJV).

➤ Being Fake: Always practice what you preach. Hold true to your convictions, and avoid getting caught with your hand in the cookie jar. Live with integrity, and be honest and fair to everyone you meet. Character matters, and integrity is important. You must live the same life in private as you do in public. If you mess up, don't back down. Come clean, and make the effort to avoid repeating the same mistake again.

➤ Avoiding Sin: When you purposely commit sin, you tempt God's grace. When you know the difference between right and wrong and you intentionally choose to transgress, God is not pleased. Fear God and respect His commandments. He is patient, longsuffering, and quick to forgive, but if you keep breaking the rules, He will throw a penalty flag your way. "Therefore, to him who knows to do good and does not do it, to him it is sin" (James 4:17 NKJV).

➢ Focusing on the Negative: Focus on being positive and being around others who will lift you up and speak life into you. No one enjoys being around people who bring them down with constant complaints and criticism. If you are like this, others will begin to avoid you and tell others to do the same. Be encouraging and upbeat so others want to be around you as you lift them up and display God's light.

➢ Judging Others: Never look down on others who may not look, act, or dress like you do. Remember that if not for the grace of God, it could be you standing on the street corner holding a cardboard sign asking for money. Be grateful to God for His blessings and give of your time and money to organizations that help to feed and clothe those in need. "Judge not, that you be not judged" (Matthew 7:1 NKJV).

Coach Bryant gave Joey Jones another chance because the young man worked hard and owned up to his mistakes. He made efforts to improve so he would not repeat his errors. When you mess up, make things right and move on. Use your blunders to learn important life lessons, and make character and integrity significant priorities in your life.

DAY 16
FOCUS ON THE KICK

November 30, 1985: Alabama 25, Auburn 23

And I am sure of this, that he who began a good work in you will bring it to completion at the day of Jesus Christ. —Philippians 1:6

The stage was set for a wild fourth-quarter finish in Birmingham, Alabama.

The Iron Bowl was living up to all the expectations of the Crimson Tide fans as Alabama took a 16–10 lead into the final period.

But the Tigers' Bo Jackson plowed into the end zone from one yard out to propel Auburn to a 17–16 lead with just over seven minutes to play in the game.

A few moments later, Alabama running back Gene Jelks romped twenty-six yards for a touchdown to retake the lead 22–17.

Auburn had a game plan to win the game that involved using up most of the time that remained. Reggie Ware culminated a seventy-yard drive that left less than a minute on the clock.

The Tigers led 23–22 because they had failed on the two-point conversion try.

Alabama needed to get within field goal range to have a chance to win, but not much time remained.

Quarterback Mike Shula connected on three passes and led the charge to the Auburn thirty-five yard line with six seconds to play.

Tide kicker Van Tiffin had one opportunity to win the game. The task ahead was enormous—a fifty-two-yard field goal.

But the Tupelo, Mississippi, native lined up the kick and focused on his mission.

The play is immortalized in Bama history as "the kick" as he cleared the uprights as time expired.

Alabama won 25–23.

Tiffin's boot through the goal posts did not merely happen. Although the play took about six seconds, it was the result of years of hard work, practice, and dedication.

But it all was worth it in the end.

> All scripture is breathed out by God and profitable for teaching, for reproof, for correction, and for training in righteousness, that the man of God may be complete, equipped for every good work. —2 Timothy 3:16–17

FAITH AND PRIDE

What tasks do you need to complete that will strengthen your Christian walk? Have you prepared yourself to come through when called upon by your team and coach? Maybe you have gone to Sunday school your entire life, but when pressed into a situation to share the gospel, can you line up the kick and deliver the good news?

AND ROLL TIDE

You need to feel confident when you take aim for the goal posts that your kick is going to be good. You might have to battle the pressure of the moment, the noise of the crowd, and other challenges to win the game. You may have prepared yourself and practiced every day for years for this opportunity, but you may only have one moment to make an impact on someone else that will change their lives forever. Here are some tips on how you can stick to the fundamentals needed to be a winning Christian on the field of play:

➤ Read Your Bible Every Day: Just like a playbook, Scripture must be studied to see results and learn how to execute each play. Don't just skim through; dive deep into the Word and allow yourself to be led by the Holy Spirit. "If you abide in me, and my words abide in you, ask whatever you wish, and it will be done for you" (John 15:7).

➤ Pray Daily: Before each game, players make sure they are ready to take the field. They eat a good meal and suit up for battle. They put on their uniform and go out as a team. They find strength in numbers. Without a rich and active prayer life, you will become weak. Build up your strength, and get on your knees every day to talk with the Lord. "Seek the LORD and his strength; seek his presence continually!" (1 Chronicles 16:11).

➤ Attend Church: A football team cannot win without playing on the field. The church is your stadium, and you need to attend it on a regular basis. What would happen if Alabama was a no-show at Bryant-Denny Stadium? They would forfeit the game and lose. If you don't attend church, the devil wins. "Not neglecting to meet together, as is the habit of some, but encouraging one another, and all the more as you see the Day drawing near" (Hebrews 10:25).

> Praise God: It doesn't matter if the ball sails through the uprights or is blocked by the opponent; raise your hands in victory. This will defeat the enemy no matter what score is posted. You win! "Bless the LORD, O my soul, and all that is within me, bless his holy name!" (Psalm 103:1).

> Serve Others: This will help you to maintain the proper perspective and promote a sense of humility. No one likes an arrogant winner. You must have a servant's heart so that when you are successful and kick the winning field goal, others will rejoice with you. Keep a pure heart and help others. Tiffin could not have kicked the winning field goal without the place holder and the linemen protecting him.

In order to be able to come through in the clutch and hit the winning points, you must be prepared and ready to go on the field when called. Put in your time and practice each day for that time when your number comes up. You never know what situation you will find yourself in with other people. Someone might need prayer or guidance on how to find Christ. Be ready for the moment.

DAY 17
SET THE TONE EARLY

October 4, 1986: Alabama 28, Notre Dame 10

He will cover you with his pinions, and under his wings you will find refuge; his faithfulness is a shield and buckler. —Psalm 91:4

Alabama Coach Ray Perkins pulled off something Bear Bryant never could during his historic and legendary career.

Perkins led the Crimson Tide to an easy win over Notre Dame.

In four tries, Bryant, who passed away in 1983, never defeated the Fighting Irish.

But on this day, the tone was set early in the first quarter, and the game was basically over after "the hit."

Perkins played for the Tide under Bryant for two years and took the job at the helm of his alma mater in 1983.

The team had bounced back in 1985 after it suffered its first losing season since 1957.

Alabama was 4–0 and ranked number two in the nation and faced 1–2 Notre Dame, coached by Lou Holtz.

This was an important opportunity to stay undefeated and knock off a storied team.

The tone of the game was established early when Notre Dame quarterback Steve Beuerlein faked a handoff and rolled right with the ball.

But Bama outside linebacker Cornelius Bennett rolled over top of Beuerlein and crushed the signal caller, sending the message that victory was near.

Beuerlein got up from the play but was hit throughout the game and completed only thirteen passes in the loss. It was later determined he suffered a mild concussion.

Alabama's offense was effective and received assistance from the special teams when Greg Richardson returned a sixty-six-yard punt for a touchdown. Quarterback Mike Shula connected on a fifty-one-yard scoring pass to Richardson for a 14–0 lead.

The Fighting Irish lost their fight. They struggled to score and failed to pose a threat to their opponent during the game.

More than 75,000 people at Legion Field knew the game was over after Bennett's bone-crushing hit on Beuerlein. It was that impressive and monumental.

The time and the score were a mere formality. The game had already been won.

> For the LORD your God is he who goes with you to fight for you against your enemies, to give you the victory. —Deuteronomy 20:4

FAITH AND PRIDE

Does your day start off on the wrong foot at times? Perhaps you are under a lot of pressure and dread the drive to work each morning. Or maybe you have an important doctor's visit coming up and are afraid to hear your test results. Life can be fun one moment and scary the next. The way you approach each new day will help you reach the end zone.

AND ROLL TIDE

How can you make an immediate positive impact? The tone you establish will set the trajectory for your day and even your life. Find a way to let people you meet know who you serve and trust. Here are some ways to be a witness of God's grace and love:

> ➢ Pray: Before any game, the coach develops a game plan and strategy to win. For you, this is accomplished with prayer before the day starts. This will allow you to be in the right frame of mind to handle any situation that might come your way. "Call to me and I will answer you, and will tell you great and hidden things that you have not known" (Jeremiah 33:3).

> ➢ Read Your Bible: The coach also selects plays from the playbook. Your instructions come from the Word of God. Study it every day before you take on the world in the field of life.

> ➢ Share Your Story: The quarterback will call out plays and signals to the offense to make sure everyone knows their assignments. You can do this too by letting others know what the Lord has done in your life. Find a way to work some news into the conversation about the goodness of the Lord and His blessings on your life. Share your story on social media or in casual discussions. You can talk about the movies, work, the weather, or vacations too, but take the opportunity when you can to mention God's part in your story. "For you will be a witness for him to everyone of what you have seen and heard" (Acts 22:15).

➤ Be Involved: You cannot make an impact on the sideline. You can cheer on your team, but you must see action to be effective. You can't catch a touchdown pass if you are not in the game. As a Christian, you need to be a part of the action by attending church on a regular basis. You can also participate in a Bible study or even start one. Get involved in a ministry or social program that is important to you. Do something to make a long-lasting impression on the lives of others.

➤ Be Positive and Happy: Attitude is everything. You cannot win unless you think you can. There is no substitute for a positive and winning outlook. Your team will only win the big game if everyone shows up ready to play. "A joyful heart is good medicine, but a crushed spirit dries up the bones" (Proverbs 17:22).

When you let people know right off the bat you are a Christian, you put them on notice. Most will respect you for taking a stand for your beliefs and will pay attention to how they act around you. When Cornelius Bennett made the hard hit, Notre Dame received the message loud and clear that Alabama was serious about winning the game. Don't keep your salvation a secret—let your colleagues and friends know you are a child of the King.

DAY 18
INTERCEPT THE UPSET BID

December 5, 1992: Alabama 28, Florida 21

Restore to me the joy of your salvation, and uphold me
with a willing spirit. —Psalm 51:12

The inaugural Southeastern Conference Championship featured
two powerhouse football teams.

The Alabama Crimson Tide (11–0) hosted Florida (8–3) at
Legion Field in Birmingham, Alabama, in hopes of going on to
play for the National Title in the Sugar Bowl.

This was the conference championship between the
champions of the SEC Western and Eastern divisions, and it
was the only way to salvage the season for the Florida Gators.

Florida jumped out to an early 7–0 lead on a five-yard
touchdown reception by Errict Rhett.

But the Tide rolled and flooded the end zone three times
in a row.

Derrick Lassic ran in from three yards out to knot the
game. In the second quarter, Curtis Brown romped in for the
score on a thirty-yard pass from quarterback Jay Barker.

Alabama extended the lead to 21–7 thanks to a fifteen-yard
bolt from Lassic.

The Gators chomped back and scored when Willie Jackson
crossed the goal line on a four-yard touchdown pass from Shane
Matthews.

Rhett tied the game with about eight minutes to play and gave momentum to the Gators. They had whipped off fourteen unanswered points and were primed to put themselves in position to win the game and upset the Tide.

With 3:16 to play in the game, Florida's quarterback dropped back to throw.

But Alabama's Antonio Langham picked off the pass and scampered twenty-seven yards into the end zone for the touchdown and the victory. He also earned game MVP honors for his heroics.

These things I have spoken to you, that my joy may be in you, and that your joy may be full. —John 15:11

FAITH AND PRIDE

Perhaps you used to live a life of happiness, joy, and peace and trusted God to take care of you. But somewhere along the way, situations in your life changed your outlook. You were cruising along and had a comfortable lead. Then the opponent scored back-to-back touchdowns. The devil would like nothing better than to drop in the pocket, connect for the long pass, and set you up for a big loss.

AND ROLL TIDE

When you know the forces of evil have developed a strategy to score, you must act fast and make the play. Step in front of the ball, intercept the attempt, and run it back for the score. Here are some tips on what not to do if you want to pick off the pass:

Day 18: Intercept the Upset Bid

➢ Worry About the Future: Depend on the Master's game plan to win the game. He knows what is in store for you. Alabama fans were nervous until Antonio Langham made the play. "Do not boast about tomorrow, for you do not know what a day may bring" (Proverbs 27:1).

➢ Agonize Over the Past: Let go of yesterday's disappointments. You cannot go back and undo what has been done. If you make a mistake, learn and grow. Be ready to make the big interception today. "Let your eyes look directly forward, and your gaze be straight before you. Ponder the path of your feet; then all your ways will be sure. Do not swerve to the right or to the left; turn your foot away from evil" (Proverbs 4:25–27).

➢ Compare Yourself to Others: You are unique and special. Never view the lives of other people and wonder what it would be like to be them. They may be hiding problems and don't show it.

➢ Focus on the Negative: Leave your troubles behind you and ask God to take care of them for you. There might be some action items for you to handle, but allow the Lord to do His work and give you another opportunity to praise Him. He never changes. "Jesus Christ is the same yesterday and today and forever" (Hebrews 13:8).

➢ Procrastinate: If Langham hesitated, he might not have made the play to win the game. Don't delay when it comes time to jump in and praise the Lord for His blessings. If He wants you to visit someone, then act promptly. If you know a person who is in need, help them. The moment may not present itself again. "If you are willing and obedient, you shall eat the good of the land" (Isaiah 1:19).

If you follow these suggestions, you may have an opportunity to develop a positive attitude and be happy. His blessings will cause you to rejoice and make the play to win. When the devil tries to go long and hit you when you are not looking, position yourself in front of the receiver and intercept the ball.

DAY 19
A GOOD DEFENSE WILL WIN

January 1, 1993: Alabama 34, Miami 13

But sanctify the Lord God in your hearts: and be ready always to give an answer to every man that asketh you a reason of the hope that is in you with meekness and fear. —1 Peter 3:15 KJV

The debut of the Bowl Championship Series National Title game pitted two undefeated teams against each other, as selected by the Bowl Coalition.

The Sugar Bowl, played in New Orleans, Louisiana, featured Alabama (12–0) versus favored Miami (11–0) for all the marbles.

Miami featured an explosive offense while the Tide counted on its defense to keep the game close.

Alabama punched first at the 10:56 mark in the opening quarter when Michael Proctor booted a nineteen-yard field goal. Miami answered with a forty-nine-yarder, and the game was tied 3–3 at the end of the period.

Proctor added another field goal in the second, which was followed by a Sherman Williams two-yard touchdown run with 6:09 to play in the half. The Tide rolled into the half with a 13–6 lead.

Alabama dominated the third quarter and scored two touchdowns within seconds of each other.

With 10:12 to go in the period, Derrick Lassic plunged in from a yard out for the score.

The next possession, Bama lined up all eleven players on the line of scrimmage, which confused Miami quarterback Gino Torretta. The move resulted in an interception by George Teague, who sprinted thirty-one yards for the score and the 27–6 lead.

This made up for an earlier play when Teague had caught up with Miami's Lamar Thomas, who was on his way for what appeared to be an eighty-nine-yard touchdown. Teague stripped the ball and took off the other way. But the play, known as "the strip," was ruled dead because of an Alabama penalty, and it prevented a Hurricane score.

Kevin Williams gave Miami a brief glimmer of hope when he returned a punt seventy-eight yards for a touchdown, but Lassic's four-yard touchdown run with 6:46 to play secured the Bama win and National Championship.

The Tide's rolling defense held the explosive offense of Miami to thirteen points.

Can you relate? Have you ever been faced against the potential offensive attacks from the devil? Did your defense rise to the occasion to help you win the game?

> I charge thee therefore before God, and the Lord Jesus Christ, who shall judge the quick and the dead at his appearing and his kingdom. —2 Timothy 4:1 KJV

FAITH AND PRIDE

Can you recall a time when your faith and beliefs came under fire? Perhaps someone at work has made fun of you for your religious convictions. Or perhaps you are challenged by people who are annoyed and jealous of the joy that is in your heart, and they look for ways to bring you down.

AND ROLL TIDE

Christians are faced with negative attacks each day. Some are mild while others can test your character and integrity. It's hard to stay calm when a person insults you or your way of life. But you need to be prepared to fight the good battle. Here are some tips to make you strong on game day and thwart off potential strikes on you for your faith:

➤ Know What You Believe: If you have experienced the grace of God, then you will know in your heart what is right and wrong. You know that you can expect to be persecuted for your beliefs. "The God of my rock; in him will I trust: he is my shield, and the horn of my salvation, my high tower, and my refuge, my saviour; thou savest me from violence" (2 Samuel 22:3 KJV).

➤ Know Your Playbook: You must spend time in the Word of God every day, even if it's only for a few moments. Plan a specific time, and honor your commitment. Keep God's Word in your heart to prepare you to respond to negative attacks. Quoting Scripture is a great weapon God gives us to use during hard times. "Open thou mine eyes, that I may behold the wondrous things out of thy law" (Psalm 119:18 KJV).

➤ Get Set on the Line of Scrimmage: Always be prepared to tell why you are a follower of Christ. You don't have to be a preacher to accomplish this. You can post inspirational messages on social media or be active in a visitation group that spreads the good news.

➢ Trust Your Defense: If you lack confidence in what you stand for, you will get run over by the devil. Put your trust in God and do your part. He will not let you down. Pray, read your Bible, and attend church on a regular basis. This is a guaranteed formula for success. "And whatsoever ye do in word or deed, do all in the name of the Lord Jesus, giving thanks to God and the Father by him" (Colossians 3:17 KJV).

➢ Make the Play: When Teague chased down the runner and took the ball away from him, the play was immortalized and even given a name. You can do the same thing. Step up and witness to someone who needs the Lord. Showing them love and kindness will strip away the negativity from those who try to bring you down.

The Miami offense entered the 1993 Sugar Bowl favored to win the game and the championship. During the season, the Hurricanes had outscored their opponents 356 to 127 with their high-scoring offense. But the Bama defense employed a strategy to limit its opponent's potential and effectiveness. The Tide rolled over and kept them from making an impact on the game. You must do the same as a follower of the Lord. Be ready to depend on God's strong defense combined with your passionate beliefs to take the sting away from the negative attacks.

DAY 20

MAKE THE MOST OF A SECOND CHANCE

October 2, 1999: Alabama 40, Florida 39

The Lord is not slow to fulfill his promises as some count slowness, but is patient toward you, not wishing that any should perish, but that all should reach repentance. —2 Peter 3:9

Florida entered the contest ranked third in the nation and held a thirty-game home-winning streak at the Swamp.

Alabama rolled into Gainesville, Florida, ranked number twenty-one and a long shot to even compete.

But they did much more than that.

The Crimson Tide sent a message that Bama football was back and a force to be reckoned with once again.

A stunned Gator crowd watched as Alabama sent the game into overtime. No one expected this to happen.

The Alabama defense forced three turnovers and converted for seventeen points.

Florida took a 33–26 lead late in the fourth quarter when quarterback Doug Johnson found Darrell Jackson for a fourteen-yard touchdown strike.

Alabama had to punt on its next possession, but Jackson could not handle it, and Marvin Brown recovered the ball for the Tide on the Gator twenty-two-yard line.

Shaun Alexander, on a fourth down, rumbled thirteen yards into the end zone and forced the overtime.

Florida gathered themselves and scored in the first overtime possession when Johnson found Reche Caldwell in the end zone for a six-yard touchdown. But Jeff Chandler missed the extra point, and the Gators led 39–33 in overtime.

Alexander once again came through for the Tide. He romped twenty-five yards, his fourth touchdown of the day, to tie the game in overtime.

All the Tide needed was the extra point.

Kicker Chris Kemp missed the attempt, and the game appeared to be deadlocked again.

But Florida's Bennie Alexander jumped offside, and Kemp got another chance. He didn't miss this time, and Alabama stunned the Gators with the upset win.

> If my people who are called by my name humble themselves, and pray and seek my face and turn from their wicked ways, then I will hear from heaven and will forgive their sin and heal their land. —2 Chronicles 7:14

FAITH AND PRIDE

Once the Lord gives you another opportunity, you must act and display a positive attitude. Forgiveness is a miraculous gift and should not be taken for granted. You can view two different opinions about the play that allowed Kemp to kick the extra point:

Miami committed a penalty or Alabama was given a second chance. What will you do when God gives you a second chance at victory?

AND ROLL TIDE

God grants forgiveness when you ask Him to. The hardest part is when you realize you must completely let go of your sin, forgive yourself, and try again. Mistakes can build up and play over and over again in your mind. Learn from them and move ahead. Don't return to your old ways, but instead remember the pain they have caused you, and use this as a motivation to win the game. Here are some tips to be victorious in overtime:

> ➤ Forgive Others First: Remember, God forgave you of your sins and washed them all away. You too must let go of things when people have hurt you. This is hard, but it's necessary to be a winner. "For you, O Lord, are good and forgiving, abounding in steadfast love to all who call upon you" (Psalm 86:5).

> ➤ Show Gratitude: Be reminded each day that Christ gave His life for you. Never forget that, and take note of the sacrifice He made for you. "Remember Jesus Christ, risen from the dead, the offspring of David, as preached in my gospel, for which I am suffering, bound with chains as a criminal. But the word of God is not bound! Therefore I endure everything for the sake of the elect, that they also may obtain the salvation that is in Christ Jesus with eternal glory" (2 Timothy 2:8–10).

> ➤ Stay Focused: Once you have dispensed of the past memories, develop a game plan that will point you to

victory. Read God's Word, pray, and seek God's will for your future.

➤ Do Something: Be willing to do whatever the Lord asks you to do for Him. If He wants you to be active in a ministry, will you obey? Can you send cards of encouragement to people or volunteer at a homeless shelter? Follow His way and determine to be an active servant for the Lord.

➤ Praise God: No matter what happens in overtime, give the Lord all the praise and glory. This can be in public, in the privacy of your home, or even on social media. He wants and deserves your praise. "Yours, O LORD, is the greatness and the power and the glory and the victory and the majesty, for all that is in the heavens and in the earth is yours. Yours is the kingdom, O LORD, and you are exalted as head above all" (1 Chronicles 29:11).

Alabama's kicker got a second chance to redeem his missed extra point and win the game. He took advantage of the opportunity. He did not pout about the missed kick—instead he focused on the task he had before him. That second chance was all he needed. God will forgive you and give you another opportunity, but you must make the most of your personal overtime period.

DAY 21
RUN HARD FOR GOD

November 20, 1999: Alabama 28, Auburn 17

Do you not know that in a race all the runners run, but only one receives the prize? So run that you may obtain it. Every athlete exercises self-control in all things. They do it to receive a perishable wreath, but we an imperishable. —1 Corinthians 9:24–25

Running back sensation Shaun Alexander decided to stay at Alabama after his junior year and forgo the NFL draft for later.

He suffered an ankle injury in a loss against Tennessee, which dashed his hopes of winning the Heisman Trophy. But he stayed the course and kept working and running to become better and stronger.

Alexander played a vital role in the Tide's 34–7 defeat of Florida during the Southeastern Conference Championship game.

But it was his performance the week before against Auburn in the Iron Bowl that the Florence, Kentucky, native was at his best.

He led a comeback and scored three touchdowns in the 28–17 grudge match. He could not be stopped and finished the game with 199 total yards.

When his college football career ended, he held fifteen records, including 3,565 yards rushing, and he was selected first-team All-American and first-team All-SEC.

In May 2011, he was inducted into the Alabama Sports Hall of Fame.

Alexander left his mark at Alabama and is remembered for giving all he could on the field for the Tide.

But I do not account my life of any value nor as precious to myself, if only I may finish my course and the ministry that I received from the Lord Jesus, to testify to the gospel of the grace of God. —Acts 20:24

FAITH AND PRIDE

The Christian race can be compared to the great career of Shaun Alexander. He was highly recruited and lived up to all expectations. Then an injury dampened his potential, but he still came back and gave an outstanding performance. He went on to enjoy a fantastic run in the NFL and was named MVP in 2005. That award goes to the athlete who excels and contributes the most to his team. He led the league in rushing for the Seattle Seahawks and was also named the most outstanding offensive player of the year. To accomplish all these achievements, he needed to be in the best physical condition possible.

AND ROLL TIDE

You face the same opponent each day when you wake up. The devil constantly orders the blitz from all sides. He will rush all of his players up the middle in hopes of a huge sack for a loss. He also wants you to fumble the ball. But your game plan must be to let God be your blockers. You must be prepared to run the pigskin right up the gut and down Satan's throat. The journey each day is not easy, and your focus must be on the Word of

God. If you stray from your game book, you might be dropped for a loss. Here are some tips to run the race hard to win:

➤ Be in Tip-Top Shape: Shaun Alexander worked out every day and was ready to play. He used his mind and body to break the defense and gain yards. Make sure you have daily devotions, attend church services when possible, and pray to the Savior often. This will make you stronger and better prepared to shake off the tacklers. "Or do you not know that your body is a temple of the Holy Spirit within you, whom you have from God? You are not your own, for you were bought with a price. So glorify God in your body" (1 Corinthians 6:19–20).

➤ Look Ahead: An effective running back does not turn his head and look behind him. He keeps his eyes focused on what is in front of him. He leaves the past behind and goes toward the end zone. When you glance back, you might become distracted from your ultimate goal and allow the defense to catch you.

➤ Surround Yourself with Likeminded People: Find friends who will encourage you and hold you accountable at the same time. Spend time with others who have the same vision and want to live right in the sight of God. If you have second thoughts about where you are going, what you are doing, and who you are doing it with, follow your gut instinct and leave. Don't wander into the other team's huddle. Expect God to bless you.

➤ Break the Chains: Do not go to places or hang with people who might bring you down. For example, if you have been delivered from a problem with alcohol, then don't go to a bar. If you struggle with gambling, stay away from casinos. Do not open yourself up to temptation. Instead, ask God to open a new pathway for you to run through. "Blessed is the man who remains steadfast under trial, for when he has stood the test he will receive the crown of life, which God has promised to those who love him" (James 1:12).

➢ Focus on the Prize: When you are running down the field of life with the ball secured, always envision the goal line. Anticipate the prize that awaits you when you score the touchdown. Every athlete wants to make that big play, and when you can see the end result, it makes your journey more fulfilling. "But our citizenship is in heaven, and from it we await a Savior, the Lord Jesus Christ, who will transform our lowly body to be like his glorious body, by the power that enables him even to subject all things to himself" (Philippians 3:20–21).

There will be times when the defense will blitz and tackle you behind the line of scrimmage. Always remember you have four downs. Huddle up, let God call the play, and allow Him to lead the charge and escort you to the end zone. Run the race.

DAY 22
YOU CAN COME BACK HOME

November 8, 2008: Alabama 27, LSU 21

Return to the LORD your God, for he is gracious and merciful, slow to anger, and abounding in steadfast love; and he relents over disaster. Who knows whether he will not turn and relent, and leave a blessing behind him, a grain offering and a drink offering for the LORD your God? —Joel 2:13–14

Alabama Coach Nick Saban returned to Tiger Stadium for the first time since he had coached Louisiana State from 2000–2004. While at the helm at LSU, he guided the Tigers to a National Championship.

But now he was the head coach at top-ranked Alabama and faced his former team, which was ranked sixteenth in the nation.

On LSU's first possession, quarterback Jarrett Lee was picked off by Bama's Rashad Johnson and returned it to the LSU fifteen-yard line.

Quarterback John Parker Wilson dove into the end zone, and Alabama led 7–0.

LSU countered as Lee found Demetrius Byrd for a thirty-yard touchdown pass to tie the game.

On the kickoff to Alabama, Javier Arenas bobbled the football, and LSU recovered on the thirty-yard line. Charles

Scott romped into the end zone, and the Tigers took a 14–7 lead.

But Johnson snagged another Lee pass and returned it for a touchdown to tie the game 14–14 at the half.

Early into the third quarter, the Tide rolled to a 21–14 lead when Glen Coffee plowed in from three yards out.

The Tigers answered and tied the game 21–21 when Scott ran the ball in for a score.

With seconds left on the game clock in the final quarter, LSU's Ricky Jean-Francois blocked a would-be game-winning field goal from Leigh Tiffin to send the game into overtime.

Alabama won the toss in overtime but elected to play defense first. This proved to be the right decision as Johnson intercepted Lee for the third time.

Wilson connected with Julio Jones on a twenty-three-yard strike to put the ball at the two-yard line. Two plays later, Wilson dove into the end zone to give Bama the win in overtime and keep the team's record spotless.

For Coach Saban, the win was a nail-biter but a successful return to his old stomping grounds.

Have you been away from your church and have a deep desire to return?

> But from there you will seek the LORD your God and you will find him, if you search after him with all your heart and with all your soul. —Deuteronomy 4:29

FAITH AND PRIDE

You can wander away from God without even realizing it. Perhaps you are enjoying your Christian walk and serving the

Lord every day. You go to church and worship the Lord and receive His blessings. Then an extracurricular activity causes you to miss a service or two, and then you sleep late and forget about your daily devotions, so you put it off until later. Then it happens again. And again. Before you know it, you are not praying, reading the Word of God, or attending church. Or maybe you are frustrated with a bad situation, and you blame the Savior for your troubles. You feel as though God has forsaken you when it is actually you who is drifting from His presence.

AND ROLL TIDE

No one chooses to deliberately backslide, but it does happen. Don't listen to the guilt trip the devil gives you; toss off the shame he tries to make you feel. Instead, realize that God offers forgiveness and love as a way to overcome the condemnation of sin. You know what you need to do, but you have hesitations. Don't wait another minute; where you spend eternity is of the highest importance. Life in Christ is fulfilling and is the only way to reach heaven. Consider these tips if you have fallen away and want to come home:

➢ Acknowledge: Recognize God is the creator of the universe, and you are a small but important creation of His plan. Be grateful for life, and remember how much He loves you and wants to welcome you back into the fold. "Know that the LORD, he is God! It is he who made us, and we are his; we are his people, and the sheep of his pasture" (Psalm 100:3).

➢ Understand: The Bible tells us that all have sinned, and this separates us from God. Remember that Christ loves you no matter what you have done. He is in control and will allow you to go through situations to teach you to depend on Him more. You are not being punished, but you are being prepared. Know the difference. "But your iniquities have made a separation between you and God, and your sins have hidden his face from you so that he does not hear" (Isaiah 59:2).

➤ Ask: You must ask the Lord for His forgiveness. If you have wronged someone, then you must make restitution too. Real repentance will develop integrity and solid character. If you have never received God into your heart, then ask Him to save you from your sins. "Repent therefore, and turn back, that your sins may be blotted out" (Acts 3:19).

➤ Seek: No one can walk this journey alone. If you drift from the pack, you will become weak and a prime victim for Satan, who is a roaring lion seeking who he may devour (1 Peter 5:8). Search for a strong, fundamental, Bible-believing church and friends who share similar convictions. Find strength in numbers and depend on them for guidance and support. It takes eleven players on the field to pull off a successful play, and it will take fellowship with other followers of Christ to stay strong.

➤ Praise: Worship God and lift your hands in thanks. He is a loving and forgiving Master, and we should never worry about what others might think. Praise Him on credit by thanking Him ahead of time for future blessings and answered prayers.

Day 22: You Can Come Back Home

Coach Nick Saban returned to LSU and kept Alabama's unbeaten season alive. You can do the same. If you have wandered away, it's time to step back on the turf and defeat the negative forces of evil that want to knock you down. Make the plays and take the win in overtime.

DAY 23
FIND HAPPINESS IN THE LORD

November 29, 2008: Alabama 36, Auburn 0

Delight yourself in the LORD, and he will give you the
desires of your heart. —Psalm 37:4

Auburn had controlled the Iron Bowl for six years straight.

But Coach Nick Saban, who took over for the Crimson Tide
in 2007, had a vision and a plan to rebuild pride in his program.

Running back Glen Coffee ran all over the Tigers for 144
yards while freshman Mark Ingram scored two touchdowns.

The Tide's defense rolled over Auburn and held them to
170 total yards.

The Tigers crossed midfield into Alabama territory one
time in the entire game.

Meanwhile, Alabama controlled all aspects of the game as
they took a 10–0 lead into the half, thanks to a thirty-seven-
yard field goal from Leigh Tiffin and a forty-one-yard romp by
Coffee.

Auburn tried to get started in the second half, but the
Alabama defense swarmed and forced fumbles on the Tigers'
first two possessions.

Tide quarterback John Parker Wilson fired a thirty-nine-
yard touchdown to Nikita Stover, and Ingram followed with a
one-yard plunge for a 22–0 lead.

Late in the third quarter, Ingram again scored on a fourteen-yard gallop, and backup quarterback Greg McElroy found Marquis Maze on a thirty-four-yard scoring strike with 2:49 to play in the game.

The Crimson Tide snapped the losing skid and played a flawless game.

Coach Saban commented after the contest that he was happy with the performance, and he even danced in the locker room.

He was also seen waving to the fans and thanking them for their support.

> And the peace of God, which surpasses all understanding, will guard your hearts and your minds in Christ Jesus. —Philippians 4:7

FAITH AND PRIDE

You may be a Christian, but life can still pull you down in the dumps sometimes. But does your outlook on life keep you from being happy? Perhaps your job has you discouraged or your doctor has delivered some news that has you worried. These are real-life scenarios. But know that no matter what you go through, you can still be happy. You don't have to enjoy the current situation, but you can choose to enjoy your ride with the Lord.

AND ROLL TIDE

True joy can only be found in the love of God, not in victories on the gridiron or in new cars or luxurious homes. You will discover the real reason to dance when you fall in love with the Lord. Look for happiness in the following:

➤ In Righteousness: "The father of the righteous will greatly rejoice; he who fathers a wise son will be glad in him" (Proverbs 23:24). You are a child of the King, and He is thrilled when you join the family of God. He loves His children, and giving your life to Him is the best choice you will ever make because He will give you true joy and peace.

➤ In Patience: "Rejoice in hope, be patient in tribulation, be constant in prayer" (Romans 12:12). Life is a marathon and not a sprint. Your journey will be long, with plenty of rewards and challenges. When you demonstrate patience with God, you allow Him to work in your life. Don't be in a hurry to take care of things your way. Let God reveal His plan to you and guide you along the way. It may take a while for you to mature and be ready. Stay in prayer and wait on the Lord. He will keep you in the palm of His hand.

➤ In Honesty: "Blessed are the pure in heart, for they shall see God" (Matthew 5:8). Always tell the truth. Maintain a pure heart, and do and say what is right in the eyes of God. Even a little white lie can grow into something big and ugly. Be true to your Lord and to yourself, and strive to show integrity in all that you do.

➤ In Peace: "Deceit is in the heart of those who devise evil, but those who plan peace have joy" (Proverbs 12:20). Maintain a spirit of peace, and do not stir up trouble. Refrain from gossip and from bearing a false witness. Walking in perfect peace with God is a wonderful thing, and spending time with Him in prayer and reading His Word brings tranquility like you've never felt before.

➤ In Love: "Let all that you do be done in love" (1 Corinthians 16:14). Loving people does not mean you allow them to take advantage and step all over you. Show the love of God to all, and let them see God's love shine through you. Treat others with kindness, and show understanding and patience even when they do you wrong. When others see how much in love you are with Christ, they will want to serve Him too.

There are many reasons to be happy when you have Jesus in your heart. Faith will help you to stay happy even when the tough trials come. When you are content in your relationship with the Master, this does not mean you will not have issues or problems. But you will be equipped to handle difficult situations better because of the joy in your heart. No matter what comes your way, you are a child of the King, and you have the best reason in the world to be happy.

DAY 24
LEARN FROM THE LOSS

December 6, 2008: Florida 31, Alabama 20

These things I have spoke unto you, that in me ye might have peace. In the world ye shall have tribulation: but be of good cheer; I have overcome the world. —John 16:33 KJV

Everyone anticipated this matchup.

The top-ranked team in the nation, Alabama, faced number-two Florida for the Southeastern Conference Championship.

The Crimson Tide rolled into the Georgia Dome 12–0 while the Gators had a record of 11–1.

It was the game of the year for fans and the media.

The hype was larger than the game itself, and both teams were total opposites.

The Florida Gators were led by Coach Urban Meyer and his quarterback, Tim Tebow. The team's unique style of fast-paced and explosive offense lined up in a spread formation most of the time and counted on speed and quickness to win each game.

Alabama was well conditioned and wore its opponents down with physical domination and hard-nosed football. Coach Nick Saban ran a down-your-throat offense and had a methodical approach to control the ball.

Florida got on the board first and took a 7–0 lead on a three-yard touchdown pass from Tebow to Carl Moore.

The Tide answered right back when quarterback John Parker Wilson hit Julio Jones on a sixty-four-yard pass that set up an eighteen-yard touchdown run by Glenn Coffee.

Bama took the 10–3 lead when Leigh Tiffin booted a field goal.

A fake field goal attempt by Alabama gave Florida good field position, allowing the Gators to tie the game on a kick of their own from thirty-one yards away.

Alabama could not get the offense going and had to punt. Soon Tebow found David Nelson on a five-yard pass to lift Florida to a 17–10 lead.

The Tide rolled back and put together its trademark drive, giving them ninety-one yards in fifteen plays that culminated when Mark Ingram went in from two yards out.

Tiffin gave the Tide the lead on a twenty-yard field goal, and the Florida offense took over.

Tebow orchestrated a long drive, and his team took the lead 24–20 when Jeffrey Demps scored on a one-yard run.

Florida put the game away on its next drive when it gained sixty-seven yards in eight plays, and the victory was sealed when Tebow hit Riley Cooper on a touchdown strike with 2:50 to go in the game.

Alabama tasted defeat but took home some valuable lessons that fueled its fire for the next year.

Fear thou not; for I am with thee: be not dismayed; for I am thy God: I will strengthen thee; yea, I will help thee; yea, I will uphold thee with the right hand of my righteousness. —Isaiah 41:10 KJV

FAITH AND PRIDE

How do you handle defeat? Alabama's players did not hang their heads and fade away. They came back the next year and knocked off Florida in the same game and went on to win the National Championship. Perhaps you worked hard for an achievement, and it was pulled out from under you like the Tide experienced. The devil will use discouragement to ruin your life and keep you from bouncing back in victory. He may use simple words said by a friend to knock you down and take you out of your game plan, or he may tackle your spirit with disappointments in your life.

AND ROLL TIDE

When you are faced with an unexpected or devastating loss, it's easy to toss in the towel and quit. But God doesn't want you to do that, nor does He expect you to. He wants you to stand up and meet your challenges with the knowledge and confidence that He provides to you in His Word. Here are some ways to battle defeat:

> ➢ Stay Close to God: When you wander off or take your eyes off God's ways, you will only find confusion. Alabama did not handle Florida's attacks and consequently fell to defeat. But Coach Saban used that game and made adjustments to ensure the loss was not repeated the following season. The Lord wants to prepare you for your next big game, and it might be sooner than you think. Keep God in the huddle at all times. "Draw nigh to God, and he will draw nigh to you. Cleanse your hands, ye sinners; and purify your hearts, ye double minded" (James 4:8 KJV).

- ➤ Remain Vigilant: Alabama let its guard down, and the Gators took over in the fourth quarter. Learn from your mistakes and losses, and be open to hear audibles from the sideline. Let the Master make adjustments, and be ready to implement the game plans.

- ➤ Be Honest: Never make an excuse for the negative things that happen to you. Accept the results and move forward. Don't dwell on what happened, but chalk it up as a lesson learned from the experience. The loss to Florida stayed fresh in the Alabama players' and coaches' minds for several months. They did not like the outcome, but they took responsibility and came back even stronger the next year.

- ➤ Stay Healthy: When you take care of yourself, you are better equipped to handle disappointments in life. This doesn't mean you turn into a health fanatic, but proper exercise combined with a healthy diet can prepare you to deal with struggles better. You must be ready mentally, physically, and spiritually at all times.

- ➤ Increase Your Time with God: When you are faced with a challenge, spend a few extra moments in your daily devotions, and seek His will and guidance. Attend church on a regular basis, and pray every day. When Alabama lost, the team went back to the game films to find out what went wrong. You need to do the same thing. Get back to the basics. "Be confident of this very thing, that he which hath begun a good work in you will perform it until the day of Jesus Christ" (Philippians 1:6 KJV).

Day 24: Learn from the Loss

Be ready to bounce back and beat the opponent. You might have some losses before you are able to win the championship. Alabama did not give up and quit after the loss to Florida. Rather, the Tide was inspired to do better the next time, and they kept their eyes on that goal until they won the National Championship. When Satan tackles you, don't run to the locker room. Get back up, and run down the field and keep fighting to reach the goal.

DAY 25
BLOCK OUT THE ENEMY

October 24, 2009: Alabama 12, Tennessee 10

Yet in all these things we are more than conquerors
through Him who loved us. —Romans 8:37 NKJV

Tennessee dominated Alabama in all aspects of the game.

The Volunteers earned twenty first downs to Alabama's sixteen and produced 339 yards of offense compared to 265.

But Alabama was better on special teams, and kicker Leigh Tiffin was four out of four, while his Tennessee counterpart, Daniel Lincoln, struggled.

The Tide rolled into the game perhaps a bit overconfident against first-year coach Lane Kiffin's squad.

But the Tennessee defense made a statement and thwarted Alabama on consecutive drives.

The Tide responded with defense of its own when Mark Barron picked off a pass from Tennessee quarterback Jonathan Crompton, which set up a thirty-eight-yard field goal from Tiffin and the 3–0 lead.

Lincoln tied the score with a twenty-four-yard field goal in the second quarter.

Tiffin connected on two attempts in the second quarter, one from the fifty-yard line and one from the twenty-two-yard line for the 9–3 halftime lead.

After a scoreless third period, the Volunteers drove to the Alabama twenty-seven-yard line and set up for a field goal.

But Terrence Cody rolled through the line for the Tide and blocked Lincoln's try.

Tiffin followed up with a forty-nine-yard field goal and increased the Bama lead to 12–3.

For the first time in his college career, Alabama running back Mark Ingram lost a fumble, and the Volunteers took over on the Tide forty-three-yard line with 3:28 to play in the game.

In just over two minutes, Tennessee marched the distance and scored on an eleven-yard touchdown pass from Crompton to Gerald Jones to cut the lead to 12–10.

Tennessee wasn't finished and pulled off the on-side kick, taking possession on its own forty-one-yard line with about two minutes to play.

The Volunteers managed to move the pigskin to the Alabama twenty-seven-yard line before Crompton spiked the ball to stop the clock with four seconds left in the game.

Lincoln had a chance to win the game and pull off the upset.

But Cody came through once again as he bullied his way through the line and blocked the field goal attempt to preserve the 12–10 win.

Cody was chosen as the Southeastern Conference Defensive Lineman of the Week while Tiffin earned Special Teams Player of the Week honors for his effective foot.

The defensive lineman came through for his team in a big way and at just the right time.

Now thanks be to God who always leads us in triumph in Christ, and through us diffuses the fragrance of His knowledge in every place. —2 Corinthians 2:14 NKJV

Day 25: Block Out the Enemy

Have you ever produced in the clutch with God's help? Have you fought a battle and the Lord led you to victory in dramatic fashion?

FAITH AND PRIDE

Perhaps you are in a struggle, and the enemy is gaining on you by bringing on pressure at work or interfering with a relationship. What can you do to halt his momentum and win the game? Ask God to help you block Satan's field goal attempts and to give you strength to stay on the winning team.

AND ROLL TIDE

You notice there is not much time remaining on the clock, and you need a big play. You have been in a struggle and need the Lord to deliver you from defeat. If you have read the Bible all the way to the end, you know that God wins, and you must remain confident that He will deliver again in this situation. Here are some tips for you to consider when you need a big play to win:

➢ Know How the Enemy Operates: The devil does not play fair. He will hit you where it hurts and hold you down as much as he can. He does not care who he hurts, and he wants to destroy you. Study your playbook, the Bible, and be consistent in your daily devotions.

➢ Be Active in Your Journey: Terrence Cody was all over the line of scrimmage and bolted through to make two tremendous plays that had a positive impact for his team. Read your Bible, pray, attend church regularly, and get involved in activities with your brothers and sisters in

Christ. Find strength in numbers to stand against Satan's helpers who want nothing more than for you to fumble and turn over your possessions to the enemy. "Be diligent to present yourself approved to God, a worker who does not need to be ashamed, rightly dividing the word of truth" (2 Timothy 2:15 NKJV).

➤ Be Ready: Alabama was not mentally prepared to play against Tennessee that day, but their training got them through. When it came down to the end, Cody found what he needed to help his team win. He was prepared for anything. He put forth the effort even when the odds were against him to block the kick. Be ready for anything the devil might toss at you.

➤ Go for the Block: Sometimes you just know what you have to do. No words are needed. If you feel a calling to visit someone in the hospital or to pay for a stranger's meal, just do it. Don't let the devil block your blessing. "For we are His workmanship, created in Christ Jesus for good works, which God prepared beforehand that we should walk in them" (Ephesians 2:10 NKJV).

➤ Celebrate and Praise Him for the Win: This is the best way to draw strength when you need it the most. When you lift your hands in praise and worship, you feel rejuvenated and invigorated. The enemy hates when you celebrate the Master's love, especially when the game is on the line. When you give God the glory for all He has done, the devil will not be able to kick the ball under the pressure.

Day 25: Block Out the Enemy

There will be days when you are not in a good mood. You are not alone; all people are prone to have a bad day now and then. But even in the darkest hour, rely on the Lord to bust through the line and make the game-saving block for you. He's ready!

DAY 26
THE DRIVE FOR SELF-CONTROL

November 27, 2009: Alabama 26, Auburn 21

A man without self-control is like a city broken into and left without walls. —Proverbs 25:28

The seventy-fourth meeting of the Iron Bowl was one for the ages.

The Auburn Tigers hosted the undefeated Alabama Crimson Tide on a Friday night.

The Tigers got off on the right foot and caught Alabama off guard by scoring two unanswered touchdowns.

Terrell Zachery went sixty-seven yards on a reverse play for Auburn for the score and then pulled off an on-side kick, recovering the ball on the ensuing kickoff.

Quarterback Chris Todd then connected with Eric Smith and, just like that, the Tigers led 14–0.

A frustrated Coach Nick Saban rallied the troops and his Tide rolled back.

With 13:26 to play in the second quarter, Trent Richardson plowed in from two yards out.

Then with 5:31 left before the half, quarterback Greg McElroy hit Colin Peek for a thirty-three-yard strike, and the game was tied.

The Tigers put a touchdown on the board in the third quarter, and Bama's kicker, Leigh Tiffin, booted two field goals to cut the lead to 21–20.

Midway through the final period, Alabama took control of the ball and marched seventy-nine yards in fifteen plays.

The drive culminated in a touchdown when McElroy found Roy Upchurch for the four-yard go-ahead score with 1:24 to play in the game.

Auburn had little time to muster up a comeback and fell short when Todd's final attempt was deflected by Alabama defenders.

To pull off the score, the Crimson Tide had to take control and play with a mission.

There was no room for mistakes, and they needed to compete with poise.

For God gave us a spirit not of fear but of power and love and self-control. —2 Timothy 1:7

FAITH AND PRIDE

Maybe you have a situation where you have to put together a lengthy drive and the odds are not in your favor. Perhaps you have been faced with circumstances where you were enticed to lose your cool, and you became angry. Or maybe you have a circumstance where you need God to appear with assurance that everything will be okay. Perhaps you need God to give you the strength to resist temptation.

AND ROLL TIDE

Self-control is a gift from the Lord. But it is also a trait you must work on and develop over time. You have to treat it like a plant, and allow water and sunlight to help it to grow. There are steps to making this happen. Alabama took fifteen plays to score. They used a methodical drive over time to achieve their goal and secure the win. You can do the same thing. Here are some tips on how to develop self-control in your situation:

> Be Honest About Your Weaknesses: The first step in overcoming your weak spots is to admit they exist. You might have a quick temper, a foul mouth, or a wondering eye. Once you recognize what is holding you back, you can address it and let God put together a drive to take you to victory.

> Join Forces: Using self-control takes a team effort. Confide in your spouse, or discuss your issues with your pastor or a mentor. This will allow them to hold you accountable and give you a resource of strength. The Alabama offense had eleven players on the field for a reason. No one player won the game. All did their job to make the drive successful.

> Set a Goal: If you know you lack in a certain area, make it a point to attack that weak spot each day. If you have a desire to stop using inappropriate language, then every time you slip up, penalize yourself with a monetary amount that you donate to your favorite charity. Chip away slowly, and let the Lord call the plays. "No temptation has overtaken you that is not common to man. God is faithful, and he will not let you be tempted beyond your ability, but with the temptation he will also provide a way of escape, that you may be able to endure it" (1 Corinthians 10:13).

> Be Determined: Alabama was faced with a few third downs in the drive but did not let that deter them.

Rather it motivated them to reach each first-down marker and keep moving forward. When you are faced with a pressure moment, have confidence and faith in the Lord that He will help you get the yards needed to move the sticks.

➤ Draw Closer: In times of struggle, the only way to reach the goal line is to let the Lord block for you and clear the path. You can do this by reading the Word of God, praying to Him each day, and being faithful in your attendance to church. Find refuge in His presence, and draw strength to win the victory. "Seek the LORD and his strength; seek his presence continually!" (1 Chronicles 16:11).

Self-control is not easy. With struggle comes temptation, and with temptation comes dependence on the Lord. To pull off a seventy-nine-yard scoring drive in the fourth quarter takes discipline and control. It also takes poise, practice, and listening to the coach. Coach Saban instilled in his players the will to win. God does the same for us and teaches us to have self-control under difficult circumstances. Roll Tide.

DAY 27
PLAY THROUGH THE PAIN

December 5, 2009: Alabama 32, Florida 13

He heals the brokenhearted and binds up their wounds.
—Psalm 147:3

In 2008, the Florida Gators dominated Alabama and squashed the Tide 31–20 to win the Southeastern Conference championship.

That loss did not sit well with Crimson Tide Coach Nick Saban, and he stewed on it all season.

The next year, both teams faced each other again in a heated rematch in Atlanta, Georgia.

Both teams were undefeated. Florida was ranked number one, and the Tide rolled in at number two in the nation.

For Alabama, revenge was not the only driving factor. A trip to the National Championship against Texas was also on the line. There was a lot riding on this game.

This matchup was the first time any conference championship game featured two unbeaten power houses.

Alabama got on the board first with 10:37 to play in the opening quarter on a forty-eight-yard field goal by Leigh Tiffin. Mark Ingram added a three-yard touchdown with 5:33 to go to increase the lead to 9–0.

A Florida field goal cut into the lead, but Tiffin answered with a boot of his own, and the Tide lead was 12–3.

The Gators came back with 4:31 to go in the half when quarterback Tim Tebow hit David Nelson for a twenty-three-yard scoring strike, and they trailed 12–10.

But Ingram countered for Bama and plowed into the end zone with 3:32 to go before intermission to expand the lead to 19–10.

A Florida field goal before the second quarter ended shrunk Alabama's lead to 19–13 at the break.

Tide quarterback Greg McElroy connected with Colin Peek at the 9:53 mark in the third for the 26–13 lead, and Ingram scored his third touchdown of the game early in the fourth quarter to put the game out of reach at 32–13.

The Tide's defense rolled over the Gators in the second and held them scoreless to preserve the win and atone for the previous year's embarrassing loss.

McElroy played an outstanding game, finishing with 239 yards passing, the selection as MVP of the game, and a couple of broken ribs.

He played through the pain and claimed victory.

Have you ever been injured during your journey? Were you able to cope with the hurt?

Gracious words are like a honeycomb, sweetness to the soul and health to the body. —Proverbs 16:24

FAITH AND PRIDE

Just because the blood of Jesus covers you does not mean your life will be a bed of tournament roses. You will still face challenges, and life may not go exactly how you anticipated. There might also be times when you are hurt by people you love. You may face a personal relationship challenge or feel helpless when someone you trusted tells a lie about you. You could face scrutiny on the job or deal with mental or physical abuse from your spouse.

AND ROLL TIDE

Everyone has been wounded at one time or another. And pain has a way of sticking around to remind you of your trials. But you must learn to let God heal you and allow you to move forward in your walk with Him. If you allow the hurt to go untreated, it can fester and make you miserable. Here are some tips on how to let Christ be your physician who is always on call:

➤ Try to Realize Why You Are Hurt: It's okay to ask God why something happened. I can remember going through difficult situations and asking the same thing. You don't have to understand the moment or circumstance, but you must come to accept that Jesus has a plan for you through all the pain. "For my thoughts are not your thoughts, neither are your ways my ways, declares the LORD" (Isaiah 55:8).

➤ Do Not Listen to the Devil: He will tell you that God has abandoned you and does not care for you. Satan will whisper this in your ear when you are weak and hurting. That is how a predator works. He will pour salt in your wound and laugh as you feel the burn and pain. During this time, it might seem easy to believe the lie, but you must be strong and know that God will deliver you. "Be strong and courageous. Do not fear or be in dread of them, for it is the LORD your God who goes with you. He will not leave you or forsake you" (Deuteronomy 31:6). In spite of the pain, you can win.

➤ Accept Help: Some people thrive on misery. Every church has its members who love to dwell on how unhappy they are. No matter what happens, they always seem to be worse off than anyone else. But you don't have be like that. When you are hurt, talk to a friend, a pastor, or, better yet, talk to God. He will hear your cries and offer a balm to heal your wounded heart. Put pride aside, and let Him cradle you in His arms.

➤ Praise Him through the Pain: Praise is the best medicine for your hurt. When you can lift your hands to worship the Lord when you are discouraged, God will bless you beyond measure. When you realize the pain and suffering you are going through is nothing compared to what Jesus went through, this will help you to glorify His name.

➤ Get Back to Work: The best way to recover is to help someone else in need. Maybe you went through a trial in order to be an inspiration to another person. Let God use your pain and suffering for His glory and honor. Allow Him to strengthen you and turn a bad situation into one that is good and empowering. "Blessed be the God and Father of our Lord Jesus Christ, the Father of mercies and God of all comfort, who comforts us in all our affliction, so that we may be able to comfort those who are in any affliction, with the comfort with which we ourselves are comforted by God" (2 Corinthians 1:3–4).

Day 27: Play through the Pain

Greg McElroy did not let anyone know that he was hurt because he didn't want to leave the game. His team needed him to rise to the occasion and deliver in the clutch. He was not about to let the previous year's defeat stop him. He played through the pain and came out a winner. You must do the same. Acknowledge your injury to yourself and God, and ignore the other team's attempts to get you to quit. Seek the help you need, and always give God the credit He is due. Then get to work and win the game.

DAY 28
MAKE THE BIG PLAY

January 7, 2010: Alabama 37, Texas 21

You are the light of the world. A city set on a hill cannot be hidden. Nor do people light a lamp and put it under a basket, but on a stand, and it gives light to all in the house. —Matthew 5:14–15

The Citi BCS National Championship was a battle between the two college football powerhouses.

Both Alabama and Texas entered the contest in Pasadena, California, undefeated.

On the first offensive drive, Texas quarterback Colt McCoy was hit hard on an option play by Alabama defensive lineman Marcell Dareus.

The 2008 Heisman trophy runner-up suffered a pinched nerve in his shoulder and could not finish the game.

Two field goals put the Longhorns ahead 6–0 early, but it came with a high cost. Their field general was out.

The Tide rolled, and the offensive line dominated the Texas front defenders.

Alabama's Mark Ingram ran wild and darted into the end zone with 14:18 to play in the second quarter, and the team took a 7–6 lead.

With just under eight minutes left in the half, freshman running back Trent Richardson bolted through the line and went forty-eight yards for the score, increasing the lead 14–6.

Then the Tide defense took over when Javier Arenas picked off a Texas pass that resulted in a field goal for Alabama and a 17–6 lead.

Right before halftime, Dareus picked off a Longhorn pass with twelve seconds left and romped into the end zone for the 24–6 lead.

Texas regrouped and scored with 1:31 to play in the third when Garrett Gilbert found Jordan Shipley for a touchdown and cut the lead to 24–13.

Then with 6:15 to play in the game, the same duo hooked up again, this time for a twenty-eight-yard touchdown, and the Tide's lead dwindled to 24–21.

Texas had the momentum and the ball deep in their own territory with about three minutes to play in the game. A long drive to score and eat the clock was the plan.

But Alabama's Eryk Anders had something else in mind. He sacked Gilbert and forced a fumble that Courtney Upshaw recovered on the three-yard line. With just over two minutes left, Ingram plowed into the end zone to grow the lead to 31–21.

With forty-seven seconds left, Richardson put the game away with a two-yard score for the win.

Two epic plays from Dareus and one from Anders had a monumental impact on the win.

Whatever you do, work heartily, as for the Lord and not for men. —Colossians 3:23

FAITH AND PRIDE

Do you want to be productive and do good things? Do you want acknowledgment for your efforts? Some people enjoy accolades and applause while others like to stay under the radar. Recognition is nice, but it should not always be the motivation behind getting something done. Dareus and Anders made impactful plays that assisted the Tide in winning the National Championship. They did it because they wanted to win. Are you satisfied to know you contribute to your team?

AND ROLL TIDE

Would you still perform at a high level if you were not mentioned or noticed by your supervisor, colleagues, or family members? Do you maintain a positive attitude and have an impact on those around you? Are you always ready to make the big play and help your team win? Here are some tips to make sure you are prepared for game day:

➢ Serve Others: Put aside your own wants and needs and focus on those people who need your help. When you take the time to help a friend through a challenging time, you can look at yourself in the mirror and be proud that you were able to make a difference. "As each has received a gift, use it to serve one another, as good stewards of God's varied grace" (1 Peter 4:10).

➢ Be Thankful: Tell God every day that you are grateful for all He has done for you. He may not give you all you desire, but He does provide your needs. Consider that blessings sometimes come when God does not give you what you ask for because He always knows what's best for you. "Giving thanks always and for everything to God the Father in the name of our Lord Jesus Christ" (Ephesians 5:20).

➤ Forgive: If you want to be successful in your journey, you must strive to have a heart of forgiveness, which is sometimes extremely difficult. When you forgive someone who has hurt you, the peace and joy in your heart will become strong. Even if someone does not apologize, forgive them so God will give you the freedom and peace you need. "But I say unto you, love your enemies and pray for those who persecute you" (Matthew 5:44).

➤ Treat Others How You Wish to Be Treated: When you can master the art of kindness and generosity toward others, even when they do not deserve it, you might be ready to enter the National Title game.

➤ Share the News: The Savior expects you to spread His Word. When Alabama won the title, Tide fans celebrated and told everyone they knew. You need to share with others about the saving grace of God. Tell everyone.

Marcell Dareus and Eryk Anders combined to make an impact for their team. You can also be ready and prepared to step on to the field to make the big plays and have a positive impact. You may not be the co-MVP like Dareus, but you can earn a robe and crown in heaven.

DAY 29
LEAVE NO DOUBT

January 9, 2012: Alabama 21, LSU 0

He gives power to the faint, and to him who has no
might he increases strength. —Isaiah 40:29

Alabama entered the 2012 BCS National Championship ranked
number two and faced off against top-ranked Louisiana State in
New Orleans.

The Tide boasted a powerful running attack and averaged
219 yards per game while only giving up 191 yards per game—
which put them at the top of the list.

On the other hand, the Tigers relied on their explosive
offense that averaged 38.4 points per game and was second in
defense with 215 yards allowed in rushing and 160 in the air.

This contest was expected to be a heavyweight matchup.

The tone was set early when LSU failed to get a first down
on the opening drive.

From that point on, the Tigers struggled to move the ball
while both defenses dug in the trenches. LSU gained one first
down and crossed the fifty-yard line once.

Three Alabama field goals gave the Tide a 9–0 lead at the half.

The second half was a mirror of the first as the Bama
defense stayed strong and controlled the high-power offense
of the Tigers.

Two more field goals boosted the Alabama lead to 15–0 at
the end of the third quarter.

Bama rolled to the game's only touchdown when Trent Richardson dashed thirty-four yards to put the game away at the 4:36 mark in the final period.

The Tide's defense rose to the occasion and provided the offense with good position throughout the game. It stayed strong, and, by the end, there was no doubt which team was better prepared to win the game and claim the National Championship.

Do people know you are a believer of Christ? Do you leave any doubt about your witness? How strong is your testimony?

> I love you, O LORD, my strength. The LORD is my rock and my fortress and my deliverer, my God, my rock, in whom I take refuge, my shield, and the horn of my salvation, my stronghold. —Psalm 18:1–2

FAITH AND PRIDE

You might be a wonderful example of what a Christian should be. You go to church, pray, and read your Bible every day. You participate in civic organizations and volunteer your time and money to charity. But do people ever hear you tell them about the love of Christ that resides within you? Are your coworkers aware that you have been washed in the blood of Jesus and that your sins are forgiven? Do you share the greatest story ever told with those around you?

AND ROLL TIDE

There are many ways you can let people know you are a child of the King without coming across as overbearing or confrontational. Some people feel the need to stand on a corner and preach at passersby while some simply do nothing to spread the news. You have a responsibility to be an ambassador for the kingdom. When you take the steps to be bold enough to let others know where you stand, you leave no doubt in their minds that you are heaven-bound. Consider these suggestions and enjoy your journey to the title in glory:

➤ Pray for Opportunities: Ask the Lord to open doors or put people in your path for you to talk with about God. Make sure you are ready to handle questions and be familiar with Scripture. You don't have to know the Word of God inside and out, but you should have a few go-to verses that can reinforce the truth.

➤ Ask God for Wisdom: You are a spokesperson for the Lord, and He wants you to tell those you meet about His goodness. But there is a time and place for these conversations. Use good judgment, and ask God to lead you to say and do the right thing that will draw others to Him and not turn them away. You can also be a witness for the Lord by simply living the Christian life in front of your colleagues every day.

➤ Use Your Personal Experience: No one can tell your story better than you, and only you can tell it from the heart. This is the best example for you to share with others because people enjoy unique stories. When the conversation comes up, explain how you changed for the better after you gave your life to Christ.

➤ Set a Goal: Commit to witnessing to one new person per week. Invite them to church or tell them about a Bible study you attend. Then increase your goals as you can.

Alabama's kicker did not become proficient at connecting on field goals without practice. The more you witness, the more comfortable you will become, and your testimony will become part of your everyday conversation.

➤ Allow It to Happen: The last thing you want to do is force your beliefs on others. But at the same time, you want to let everyone know about God's love. If you are involved in a chat with someone, find ways to mention your Lord during the conversation. If someone asks about your weekend, tell them it was fantastic and that you went to a wonderful church service. If you are asked about your plans for the evening, slip in that you plan to spend it with your family and go to a Bible study. Then ask them what their plans might be. Let it flow into the dialogue from there, and capitalize on every opportunity you get to tell others about what God has done for you.

Alabama took advantage of an early miscue from LSU that set the tone for the game. From then on, everyone knew the Tide was going to roll to the win. They executed the game plan and took home the trophy. Practice makes perfect, and witnessing makes you stronger and lets others know that you take a stand for Christ.

DAY 30
DON'T LET THE TIME RUN OUT

December 1, 2012: Alabama 32, Georgia 28

The soul of the sluggard desireth, and hath nothing: but the soul of the diligent shall be made fat.
—Proverbs 13:4 KJV

Alabama entered the conference championship game ranked second in the nation, while Georgia was right behind them at third. Both teams were 11–1, and the winner would face Notre Dame for the national title.

Neither team scored in the first quarter.

But the Georgia Bulldogs had to mix it up a bit and used a fake punt to convert a fourth down, which led to a nineteen-yard touchdown pass.

The Tide rolled back when Eddie Lacy romped forty-one yards for a touchdown, and that was followed by a Ha Ha Clinton-Dix interception that resulted in a Jeremy Shelley field goal and a 10–7 lead at the break.

Georgia came out in the third on a mission.

One of the two touchdowns they scored came off a blocked field goal and ended with a fifty-five-yard return by Alec Ogletree.

Alabama responded when T. J. Yeldon dashed into the end zone, and that was followed by another Lacy touchdown run to end the third quarter.

Both Bama backs finished the game with at least 150 yards rushing, which was the first tandem to accomplish this feat.

On the next drive, the Bulldogs took the lead again when Todd Gurley scored on a touchdown run.

The Tide got the ball with 5:24 to play in the game and trailed by three.

Quarterback A. J. McCarron saw the defense stacked up at the line and completed a pass to Amari Cooper for a forty-five-yard touchdown strike.

Georgia had one drive left.

With nine seconds left on the clock and the ball at the Alabama eight-yard line, Georgia quarterback Aaron Murray's pass was deflected toward Chris Conley, who caught the ball and fell to the turf at the five-yard line.

The Bulldogs had no time outs left, and the clock ran out. Alabama won the game and the SEC Championship.

Have you found yourself close to the goal with a chance to win but time expired? Maybe you have good intentions but never reach the end zone? Why?

> The hand of the diligent shall bear rule: but the slothful
> shall be under tribute. —Proverbs 12:24 KJV

FAITH AND PRIDE

Life is busy, and unexpected events steal your time and leave you with unfulfilled promises. It's easy to become distracted, and your mind can shift in thirty different directions in an hour. Maybe you want to visit a friend who is dejected, and you just forget. Or maybe you want to attend your child's after-school function and your boss gives you another work assignment. Or perhaps you want to rekindle a relationship or become more involved in a charity.

AND ROLL TIDE

No matter what you want to do or are called to do by the Lord, there is no time like now to begin. You have one drive left, and the clock is ticking. You don't have any timeouts left, and you are playing for a trip to play for the title. Will you make the play or fall down just shy of the goal and let the clock run out on your journey? Here are some tips to make sure you get into the end zone:

➢ Don't Procrastinate: Act now. If you have put off telling someone you love them, there is no better moment than today. Maybe your parents are old, and you haven't expressed your feelings to them in a long time. Go tell them. Or maybe you have put off going to a special charity event. Go and get involved. Don't wait and be denied a blessing by being a help to someone who might need you. "Boast not thyself of to morrow; for thou knowest not what a day may bring forth" (Proverbs 27:1 KJV).

➢ Help Someone out of a Bind: If a friend reaches out to you and needs a favor, don't look the other way or try to get out of the situation. Put yourself in their shoes and be a blessing. "Thine own friend, and thy father's friend, forsake not; neither go into thy brother's house in the day of thy calamity: for better is a neighbor that is near than a brother far off" (Proverbs 27:10 KJV).

➢ Give Roses While You Can: Send a note of encouragement to a friend or brag on someone who means a lot to you.

This can be done in a church service or in a public meeting. Let them know they are appreciated for their sacrifices. Don't wait to put flowers on their grave. Tell them today.

> Take Your Spouse Out on a Date: It's easy to take someone for granted and assume they know how you feel. Make it a point to treat the person you love to a special night now and then. Send a note or card for no reason, and let them know how important they are to you. If you don't have someone in your life, then do this for your pastor or a mentor.

> Spend Time with Loved Ones: The extra hours spent at the office or on social media can wait. If you have young children who desire your attention, give it to them now. They will not be young long, and once these opportunities are gone, you will never get them back. If your kids are older and you neglected to spend time with them because of other obligations, make up for it today. Become involved in their lives, and don't let time run out.

When you take a moment to make others feel special, you take advantage of the most precious resource you will ever have—time. Imagine how the outcome might have been different had Georgia had one time out left with the ball on the five-yard line. They squandered an opportunity, and Alabama was the victor. Don't let valuable time pass you by.

DAY 31
WATCH FOR THE PENALTIES

January 7, 2013: Alabama 42, Notre Dame 14

For God has not given us a spirit of fear, but of power and of love and of a sound mind. —2 Timothy 1:7 NKJV

The Crimson Tide sent the message early in the 2012 BCS National Championship game that they meant business.

Alabama, fresh off the Southeastern Conference Championship with a win over Georgia, faced number-one ranked Notre Dame in Miami, Florida.

The Tide rolled on the first drive and marched eighty-two yards in five plays for the score when Eddie Lacy dashed twenty yards for the score and the 7–0 lead.

Notre Dame's first drive stalled, and Alabama forced them to punt.

The Fighting Irish seemed to catch a break when Alabama's Christion Jones fumbled the kick and Notre Dame recovered.

But a kick-catching penalty was called on Notre Dame, and the Tide was awarded the ball. This is when the player receiving the kick is interfered with prior to catching the ball.

Alabama drove sixty-one yards in ten plays and scored when quarterback A. J. McCarron hit Michael Williams for a three-yard touchdown pass and the 14–0 lead.

The Crimson Tide took a commanding 21–0 lead when they marched eighty yards and T. J. Yeldon scored on a one-yard run.

With thirty-one seconds left in the half, McCarron found Lacy for an eleven-yard touchdown, and Alabama took a 28–0 lead into the break.

Everyone knew the game was over.

But Notre Dame had some pride left and managed to score two times while Alabama added to the lead when McCarron connected with Amari Cooper on a thirty-four-yard touchdown strike.

The final Tide score featured the duo of McCarron and Cooper again, this time on a nineteen-yard pass that concluded a fourteen-play, eighty-six-yard drive.

Lacy finished the game with 140 yards rushing, and Yeldon tossed in 104 yards on the ground.

McCarron established himself as Alabama's all-time leader in touchdown passes with forty-nine.

Notre Dame's early penalty for interfering with Jones as he attempted to field the punt set the tone for the entire game. Alabama took advantage of the opportunity and scored because of the mistake.

The devil will try to force you to fumble every time, and you must be aware of his tactics.

The LORD is my light and my salvation; whom shall I fear? The LORD is the strength of my life; of whom shall I be afraid? —Psalm 27:1 NKJV

FAITH AND PRIDE

Satan and his team do not play fair. They will kick and scream and try to make you mess up. They will instruct others to lie about you to damage your reputation and try to exploit your weaknesses. The devil and his players will wait for the perfect time to cause a rift between you and your spouse. Or they will plant seeds of discouragement and wait for them to grow.

AND ROLL TIDE

When you are a Christian, you are not exempt from facing troubles. The devil will not go after something he already possesses. He wants your soul, and he will not rest until he makes you drop the kick and surrender the ball to him. There is no such thing as a "fair catch" in life. You must be prepared for the tricks from the other team. Here are a few strategies the devil uses to try to bring you down:

➤ Fear: This is one of his go-to plays. If the devil can cause you to fear and doubt, then he has a slim chance to win the series. This can be the result of a job loss or a family illness. Or it can come about through a personal relationship problem. Fear can grip you and take over your thoughts. Give your fears to God, and ask Him to replace them with hope. Kick the fear away, and rejoice in the Savior's love for you. "For I, the LORD your God, will hold your right hand, saying to you, 'Fear not, I will help you'" (Isaiah 41:13 NKJV).

➤ Discouragement: Satan and his minions love this one. They work to slip disappointment into your life to try to take away your desire to read your Bible or go to church.

Untruths can take the wind right out of your sails. A job layoff can test your reliance on God, and a disturbing medical diagnosis can leave you with questions for the Lord. This is exactly what the devil wants. He desires to deflate your trust in the Lord and tries to make you think God has deserted you. But Christ can offer the opposite. He can rescue you from Satan's traps and help you realize just how blessed you are. God can change your perspective and help you focus on the positive. Watch out for the devil's tricks of discouragement as they are disguised well. Instead, take hope in Jesus. "Peace I leave with you, My peace I give to you; not as the world gives do I give to you. Let not your heart be troubled, neither let it be afraid" (John 14:27 NKJV).

➤ Worry: What a waste of time. You can't control what will happen tomorrow or what took place yesterday. But this trap of the devil is an easy one to fall into. This doesn't mean you stop caring about things, but why waste your time worrying about circumstances beyond your control? Do what you can on your part and follow God's will, and then turn the situation over to God and trust His plan. "And which of you be worrying can add one cubit to his stature?" (Luke 12:25 NKJV).

➤ Separation: The devil will try to bring division into your life. He wants to separate you from your family, the church, and the Lord. He will not rest until he accomplishes this task. He will try little things like enticing you to play golf on Sunday morning instead of going to church. Or he will make sure you work late when your son or daughter has an important school function. He will try to get you to put everything ahead of God. But stand strong, and make sure that taking your family to the house of God is a top priority.

➤ Temptation: This is the oldest trick in the book. The devil will place obstacles in your life that might appear to be attractive. This could be another job that could take you away from your family or church, or he might pull out the big guns and toss another person into your life to try to break up your family. The bells and whistles are there, but you cannot let them distract you. Run from evil and abstain from the very appearance of it. Take on the armor of God, and ask Him to protect you from the destruction Satan has planned for you and your family. "And do not lead us into temptation, but deliver us from the evil one. For Yours is the kingdom and the power and the glory forever. Amen" (Matthew 6:13 NKJV).

For the glory of God, you must stay alert to Satan's tricks and throw the flag to enforce illegal infractions against him. Christ will penalize the forces of evil and award you the ball. He will then call the right plays and allow you to march down the field and score the touchdown to take control of the game.

DAY 32
OVERCOME ADVERSITY

November 8, 2014: Alabama 20, LSU 13

And we know that for those who love God all things work together for good, for those who are called according to his purpose. —Romans 8:28

The annual rivalry game was more tense than usual.

Alabama, ranked fifth in the nation, entered Baton Rouge, Louisiana, to take on Louisiana State, ranked sixteenth.

Neither offense could find a rhythm, and both teams traded punts for the first several possessions.

The Tigers got on the board first when quarterback Anthony Jennings found Malachi Dupre for a fourteen-yard touchdown and the 7–0 lead.

The Tide had a chance to narrow the gap but missed a twenty-seven-yard field goal toward the end of the first quarter.

But Alabama came back and tied the game when Blake Sims fired a twenty-three-yard touchdown pass to Amari Cooper early in the second quarter.

With about a minute to play in the half, Eddie Jackson intercepted a pass for the Crimson Tide and returned the ball to the LSU twenty-nine-yard line.

Adam Griffith did not miss his next field goal attempt, this one from thirty-nine yards out, and Bama led 10–7 at the break.

The Tigers tied the game 10–10 on a thirty-five-yard field goal off their first drive of the second half.

Both teams stalled on offense until one minute remained in the final quarter.

The Tigers forced a fumble from T. J. Yeldon and recovered it on the Bama six-yard line.

An unsportsmanlike conduct call and a pair of short gains allowed LSU to kick a field goal to put them ahead 13–10.

But the Tide caught a break when the kickoff went out of bounds and gave them decent field position with seconds left on the clock.

Sims drove the offense to their own fifty-five-yard line and converted on two third downs while scrambling for the markers.

Griffith tied the game on a twenty-seven-yard field goal to force overtime.

The Crimson Tide scored and took the 20–13 lead when Sims found DeAndrew White on a six-yard pass in the end zone.

LSU could not score and fell to Alabama.

If you faint in the day of adversity, your strength is small. ——Proverbs 24:10

FAITH AND PRIDE

Life is full of challenges. Some are manageable while others can take you to your knees. No matter how big or small your obstacle may be, it's important to you nonetheless. You may be faced with a health concern that caught you off guard, or you might be having issues with your boss or a coworker. You might be in college dealing with strong peer pressure or experiencing difficulty getting good grades. Or you might be going through a relationship struggle.

AND ROLL TIDE

You are not alone. Everyone has problems. Alabama faced two separate obstacles in the game against LSU. The first one was when they missed the field goal to tie the game. The Tide responded and converted on their next attempt for three points. The second challenge came when T. J. Yeldon fumbled, and that was followed by the unsportsmanlike conduct call. Alabama came back and forced overtime with a field goal with seconds to play. Both times the Crimson Tide came back and did not let the situation overtake them. Your life is not a football game, but how you handle problems will reveal your character. Try these suggestions to help you cope with daily unpleasant circumstances:

> ➤ Avoid Self-Pity: When you entertain the attitude that you "can't catch a break" or that you are going through a "stretch of bad luck," you must change gears quickly. Everyone goes through challenges in life. But you must take the view that God has a big plan for you, and He wants to work in you and let His light shine through your testimony. When you allow bitterness or self-pity into the room, they will make themselves at home. Kick them out.

> ➤ Believe in the Goodness of the Lord: When you are discouraged, try to find inspiration in ordinary things. For example, if God can make a firefly light up at twilight, He can take care of you. If He can feed a sparrow, God can

take care of you. "Surely goodness and mercy shall follow me all the days of my life, and I shall dwell in the house of the LORD forever" (Psalm 23:6).

➤ Look Back and Be Thankful: You may not have all you desire, but you possess all you need. Perhaps God has said no to some things you wanted because He knew this was in your best interest. Perhaps you were passed over for a job because He has a better one for you down the road. Show appreciation for where you are today and where you could have been. That will help you through the difficult times. "Through him then let us continually offer up a sacrifice of praise to God, that is, the fruit of lips that acknowledge his name" (Hebrews 13:15).

➤ Be Determined: Adam Griffith missed a field goal early in the game but was determined to do better the next time on the field. He did not reflect back on his mistake but took advantage of the opportunities to come through. You must do the same. Forget the mistakes of the past and be positive that you will come through when called upon. All you have to do is be the placeholder and set the ball for the Lord to kick it through the uprights. Have confidence because you are a child of the King, and you know how the game will end.

➤ Be Happy: Laugh more, especially at yourself. Don't take yourself too seriously or be overconfident with pride. When you can smile in the face of adversity and laugh when things go wrong, you admit there is a higher power in control of your life. Go along for the ride and enjoy God's sense of humor. "Therefore my heart is glad, and my whole being rejoices; my flesh also dwells secure" (Psalm 16:9).

Mistakes will happen. You are not perfect. Be adaptable and recognize life will throw you for a loss at times. But when you have the right attitude and let God know the game situation, He will score the winning touchdown in overtime for the big win.

DAY 33
MAKE THE RECEPTION

November 29, 2014: Alabama 55, Auburn 44

And that, knowing the time, that now it is high time to awake out of sleep: for now is our salvation nearer than when we believed. —Romans 13:11 KJV

Both teams fired on all cylinders, and the scoreboard lit up like a Christmas tree.

Early in the first period, Alabama took a 7–0 lead against Auburn when T. J. Yeldon crossed the goal on an eight-yard run.

The Crimson Tide added to its lead when Amari Cooper caught a seventeen-yard touchdown pass from Blake Sims that made the score 14–3.

But the Tigers rallied when they scored a touchdown and added a pair of field goals to take a 16–14 lead.

Yeldon put the Tide back up on top 21–16 when he dove in from a yard out.

Auburn then scored ten points to take a 26–21 halftime lead.

The lead grew for the Tigers in the third quarter 33–21, but the Tide answered on a thirty-nine-yard scoring strike from Sims to Cooper.

After an Auburn field goal, the Tide rolled and scored on their next four possessions, which included a seventy-five-yard touchdown pass from Sims to Cooper.

Cooper tied the school single-game record with thirteen receptions, twenty-two yards receiving, and three touchdowns as Alabama won the Iron Bowl 55–44. It was perhaps his finest game in his three-year career with the Crimson Tide.

The junior from Miami, Florida, set records at the University of Alabama. He hauled in 224 yards catching in two different games and finished the season with 124 receptions for 1,727 yards and 16 touchdowns.

He established himself as the all-time leader in school history with 229 catches for 3,463 yards and 31 total touchdowns.

Cooper's talent to receive the ball made him a first-round draft pick in the NFL.

Will you catch what the Holy Spirit will throw at you? Will you receive the pass of salvation?

> For he saith, I have heard thee in a time accepted, and in the day of salvation have I succoured thee: behold, now is the accepted time; behold, now is the day of salvation. —2 Corinthians 6:2 KJV

FAITH AND PRIDE

Once you accept Jesus into your heart, seek God's will to go to the next level in your Christian journey. Don't settle to be an average child of the King when something inside of you wants to reach higher. Seek God's will in your life and know He will equip you to do what He calls you to do. You can soar to new heights, but you must seek Him in prayer and allow His spirit to guide you.

AND ROLL TIDE

It's time to play with the big boys of the SEC. Perhaps you are convicted now and want to ask God to take you higher in your relationship with Him. Amari Cooper carried on the tradition of winning football with the Crimson Tide, and now it's your turn to receive the Holy Spirit and step up to the next level in your walk with Christ. Here are some suggestions on how you can receive what the spirit has for you and live a more productive life for the Lord:

➢ Through the Word of God: Let the Holy Spirit speak to you and move you through Scripture. Cooper had to know the playbook, and so do you. Invest your time to study the Bible to help you find your path and direction. "Study to shew thyself approved unto God, a workman that needeth not to be ashamed, rightly dividing the word of truth" (2 Timothy 2:15 KJV).

➢ Through the Church: Take advantage of the home field crowd and receive their encouragement and inspiration. Establish yourself and your family in a church where you feel welcomed. Become involved, and don't be content to sit on the sidelines. Do whatever is asked of you, and put your ego aside. If you want to lead the singing but the church needs a van driver, then grab the keys and go to work for God.

➢ Through Your Giving: You are commanded to give back a portion of what the Lord has given you. Your gift or tithe is more than just reaching into your pocket and tossing a few dollars into the offering plate. It should be a time of worship, and you should feel happy to be able to honor the Savior with your tithe. He doesn't need your money, but you need His blessings. "Bring ye all the tithes into the storehouse, that there may be meat in mine house, and prove me now herewith, saith the LORD of hosts, if I will not open you the windows of heaven, and pour you out a blessing, that there shall not be room enough to receive it" (Malachi 3:10 KJV).

➢ Through Your Circumstances: If you can maintain a sense of humility through your life struggles and successes, then you will be better equipped to entertain the Holy Spirit within you. There is no room for the Lord's presence and self-pride to coexist. You may possess three cars and two houses, or perhaps you use public transportation and live in a government-subsidized apartment. If you put God first in your life, He will take care of your needs, and you will be blessed.

➢ Through Your Praise: This is the big one. If you are able to give thanks and praise to the Lord through all things, you will be in the Spirit. He expects you to worship Him through both the good times and bad. Everyone has problems and trials as well as successes and failures. He never promised a 55–0 shutout of the devil, but He did give His word that He will provide for you. Thank Him every day in all circumstances.

These things are not as hard as hauling in a touchdown catch from Blake Sims, but they will give you more than a win at the Iron Bowl or a championship SEC title will ever provide for you. Instead of being a finalist for the Heisman Trophy, you will receive a robe and crown and be proclaimed a National Champion when you enter heaven.

DAY 34

TODAY IS YOUR DAY OF SALVATION

December 6, 2014: Alabama 42, Missouri 13

For he says, "In a favorable time I listened to you, and in a day of salvation I have helped you." —2 Corinthians 6:2

Alabama entered the Southeastern Conference Championship game favored by two touchdowns.

On the other end, Missouri (10–2) had slim hopes of pulling off the upset but was satisfied to be in the contest.

This was the ninth time the Tide rolled into the title conference championship, and they were 4–4 in previous matchups.

The Missouri Tigers boasted a strong pass defense, but it did not hold up against Alabama's offensive wave, which steamrolled the front of the Missouri defensive unit and used short passes to pick apart the secondary to set up a fierce rushing game.

Bama running back T. J. Yeldon popped into the end zone from one yard out with 11:24 to go in the first quarter for the 7–0 lead.

A few seconds later, quarterback Blake Sims connected with DeAndrew White for a fifty-eight-yard touchdown strike, and the Tide rolled to a 14–0 lead.

Yeldon added another touchdown toward the end of the second quarter, and Alabama had a 21–3 lead.

Missouri was able to put ten more points on the board in the third but was no match for its opponent's high-powered offensive attack.

Sims then found Christian Jones on a six-yard touchdown strike with 14:55 to play in the final quarter for the 28–13 lead.

Derrick Henry then sprinted twenty-six yards with 7:38 remaining and followed with a one-yard touchdown run for the 42–13 win.

Sims, who had been under scrutiny during the regular season, was named the MVP of the game. He connected on twenty-three of twenty-seven passes for 262 yards and two touchdowns. He also completed 85 percent of his passes, which established an SEC Championship game record.

This was his day in the sun and his time to shine.

> Besides this you know the time, that the hour has come
> for you to wake from sleep. For salvation is nearer to
> us now than when we first believed. —Romans 13:11

FAITH AND PRIDE

Are you a follower of Jesus Christ? If not, do you have family and friends who pray for you each day to make the choice and accept His plan of salvation? Or maybe you have felt the conviction of the Holy Spirit, and you know what you must do to be saved, but you haven't yet made this decision. When you make the choice to ask Jesus into your heart and live the best life ever, it will be the best life-changing play you will ever make. You can live a meaningful and fulfilled life that will impact others every day.

AND ROLL TIDE

Blake Sims enjoyed one of the best days in his college career in the SEC Championship game. He kept his calm and stayed with the game plan, even though he faced criticism throughout the season. He knew his mission and focused on the prize. If you are a nonbeliever and want to claim your day as MVP, follow these suggestions:

➤ Recognize Your Need for Christ: Without the Lord, there is no hope. People might try to substitute other things to fill a void, but the emptiness will always be there. When you turn to Jesus, you can be happy and live with joy and peace in your heart. "For the wages of sin is death, but the free gift of God is eternal life in Christ Jesus our Lord" (Romans 6:23).

➤ Believe in the Virgin Birth: You must trust that the Christ child came into this world pure, undefiled, and conceived by the Holy Spirit. He was both God and man, lived a perfect and sinless life, and came to earth to provide salvation for humankind. Through his shed blood on the Cross, we can find forgiveness of our sins. "Behold, the virgin shall conceive and bear a son, and they shall call his name Immanuel" (Matthew 1:23).

➤ Believe Christ Died on the Cross and Rose the Third Day: Jesus Christ was crucified on a cross for your sins and died so you can have everlasting life. He was placed in a borrowed tomb and arose from the grave on the third day. Take comfort in this fact and know that He will return someday to take His children home to live with Him in heaven for eternity. "If the Spirit of him who raised Jesus from the dead dwells in you, he who raised Christ Jesus from the dead will also give life to your mortal bodies through his Spirit who dwells in you" (Romans 8:11).

➢ Ask Him to Forgive You and Submit to Him as Your Lord and Savior: Accept His offer of salvation, confess your sins to the Lord, and ask for His forgiveness with a repentant heart and a contrite and humble spirit. Believe that He can forgive you and cleanse you from all unrighteousness. He has the power to make you a new person and give you a whole new lease on life. "For God so loved the world, that he gave his only Son, that whoever believes in him should not perish but have eternal life" (John 3:16).

➢ Serve Him and Give Praise: After you have made the choice to live for Him, read and study God's Word each day to understand how to live the Christian life. Pray, go to church, and serve others with a grateful heart. "Praise the LORD! Oh give thanks to the LORD, for he is good, for his steadfast love endures forever!" (Psalm 106:1).

Sims earned his day in the sun. He played well and made the most of the opportunities to win. After you accept Christ as your Savior, make the most of God's blessings in your life, and try to learn as much as you can about serving Him. Move forward, and don't retreat to your old ways of sin and destruction. Take a stand, and live for the Lord. Make today your day of salvation!

DAY 35
DON'T TAKE GOD FOR GRANTED

January 1, 2015: Ohio State 42, Alabama 35

For the protection of wisdom is like the protection of money, and the advantage of knowledge is that wisdom preserves the life of him who has it. ——Ecclesiastes 7:12

The eighty-first Sugar Bowl featured the first-ever College Football Playoff semifinal game between number-one Alabama and number-four Ohio State.

The Ohio Buckeyes entered the game with a third-string quarterback fresh off a 59–0 thumping of Wisconsin to win the Big Ten Championship, which propelled them into the playoffs.

Cardale Jones had started one game when he was suddenly thrust into the spotlight for a chance to advance to the National Championship.

But the top-ranked Crimson Tide stood in his way.

The Buckeyes started a drive from their own fifteen, which resulted in a 3–0 lead.

OSU's Ezekiel Elliott lost his first fumble of the year, and the Tide rolled over the ball.

Derrick Henry gave Alabama a 7–3 lead when he went twenty-five yards for the touchdown.

Another field goal by Ohio State cut the lead 7–6.

Blake Sims later found Amari Cooper for a fifteen-yard touchdown pass, and Alabama led 14–6.

Alabama added another touchdown when T. J. Yeldon went from a yard out after the defense picked off a Jones pass.

The Buckeyes came back when Elliott scored from three yards out to cut the lead 21–13.

With a few seconds left in the half, OSU closed the gap on a trick play that saw wide receiver Evan Spencer throwing a pass to Michael Thomas for a touchdown to put them on the heels of the Tide with a score of 21–20.

Ohio State had dominated and outgained the Tide 348 yards to 139.

But there was one more half to go.

In the third, Jones fired a rocket to Devin Smith for a forty-seven-yard strike, and the Bucks led 27–21.

The Buckeye defense stiffened and picked off a Sims pass and returned it for a score, and their lead grew to 34–21.

Right before the third quarter ended, Alabama kept their hopes alive by scoring to put the game at 34–28.

Then disaster happened when Elliott broke through the line and outran everyone for an eight-five-yard touchdown and the 42–28 lead.

Bama fought back and scored with 1:59 to play when Cooper caught a pass from Sims to stay in the game 42–35. But the Tide got the ball back without any timeouts left and little time remaining.

But Sims's final pass into the end zone was intercepted, and Ohio State advanced to the National Championship game.

The Buckeyes beat Alabama with a third-string quarterback. Some commentators suggested the Tide might have taken the contest for granted, although Bama faithful knew this was not the case.

Have you ever taken your blessings and relationship with God for granted?

> May the God of hope fill you with all joy and peace in believing, so that by the power of the Holy Spirit, you may abound in hope. —Romans 15:13

FAITH AND PRIDE

Maybe you are happy with your life and on top of the world. But if you are not careful, you can overlook the attacks from the enemy and get caught off guard. A simple insignificant problem could turn into a third string quarterback and throw you for a loss.

AND ROLL TIDE

When you don't take the devil seriously, you can fall into his trap. Although you appear to be a strong follower of the Lord, the demons know how to find your weakness. You might roll into a situation ranked number one, but before you know it, you find yourself down on the scoreboard. Your relationship with God must be at the top of your game play each day. Never take your salvation for granted, and never take the following for granted:

> ➤ God's Love: Your Heavenly Father cares so much for you that He sent His Son to die for your sins. Never assume you are worthy of this gift. By His grace, you can live an abundant life and tell others about the plan of salvation.

Don't take His love for granted. "For God so loved the world, that he gave his only Son, that whoever believes in him should not perish but have eternal life" (John 3:16).

➤ Your Life: This gift is unique to you. Be thankful for each day you are alive and healthy. Make the most of your opportunity to live your life as a Christian. Make sure you are an ambassador for the kingdom, and never pass an opportunity to tell those close to you how much you love them. Protect life from the womb to the tomb. Don't take your life or anyone else's for granted.

➤ Forgiveness: This is one of God's greatest gifts to you. But don't take it lightly and treat it like a genie in a bottle by willfully sinning so you can seek forgiveness later. Appreciate and revere the great sacrifice Jesus made for you when He died on the Cross to atone for your transgressions. He has thrown your sins into the sea of forgetfulness. If He can forgive you, then you can certainly forgive others. Don't take His compassionate mercy for granted.

➤ The Holy Spirit: This is the comforter in your life. The Holy Spirit guides you every day to do what is right. Welcome the presence of the Lord into your life, and always listen to its still small voice. Keep the Spirit with you, and never hinder it to leave you. Be sensitive, and never take the Spirit of God for granted. "Now the Lord is the Spirit, and where the Spirit of the Lord is, there is freedom" (2 Corinthians 3:17).

➤ Your Gift: You have one. Everyone does. You may not be the best singer or preacher of the Word. Your gift may not ever be noticed by a crowd. If you are blessed with the

Day 35: Don't Take God for Granted

ability to write, then pursue it. If your gift is thoughtfulness, then send cards to people. Maybe you are a prayer warrior. If you do not use your gift for His glory, He may take it away. Your gift might seem small to you, but it could be life changing for others. Use your gift. Don't take it for granted.

Ohio State came ready to play and was deep in talent. It was their night to win, and they proved all the analysts wrong by winning the National Championship. In my opinion, the Tide may have taken OSU for granted. Make sure you keep your defenses up at all times, and always stay prepared to win.

DAY 36
SACK THE ENEMY

October 24, 2015: Alabama 19, Tennessee 14

But you, take courage! Do not let your hands be weak,
for your work shall be rewarded. —2 Chronicles 15:7

Alabama and Tennessee were tied 7–7 at the break.

The Crimson Tide came out in the third quarter and put together a lengthy twelve-play drive that went seventy-three yards and resulted in a nineteen-yard field goal to push the score 10–7 with nine minutes left in the quarter.

Tennessee had three opportunities to score throughout the game and missed field goal attempts, one from forty-three yards and two from fifty-one yards.

These would have kept Tennessee in the game and given them a lead at one point.

With 14:06 to play in the fourth quarter, Alabama marched fifty-six yards in twelve plays and chewed up almost seven minutes of time.

During the drive, Bama faced a third-down and eleven yards to go at the Tennessee forty-six-yard line with 10:19 to play. Quarterback Jake Coker found ArDarius Stewart for a fifteen-yard completion to move the markers.

The Tide was rolled back ten yards on a penalty and faced first-down and twenty.

Coker connected to Calvin Ridley for twenty-six yards and moved the ball to the Tennessee fifteen-yard line inside the Red Zone.

The ball was thrown a little behind Ridley, and he adjusted his body to grab the pass and gained more yards on the ground after the catch.

Running back Derrick Henry was thrown for a loss, and Alabama faced another third down and six at the UT eleven-yard line.

The Tide settled for a twenty-eight-yard field goal and a 13–7 lead with 7:08 to play. Still too close for comfort.

Tennessee responded and marched back and grabbed a 14–13 lead in four plays that gained seventy-five yards.

Tailback Jalen Hurd scored on a twelve-yard run but left 5:49 on the clock.

Alabama had the ball and faced a second down and eleven at their own twenty-seven-yard line. Coker found Stewart again, this time for a twenty-seven-yard completion with 4:29 to play.

Moments later, it was third down and six when Coker found Ridley, who leaped over a Volunteer defensive back to make a spectacular catch and move the chains.

A few plays later, Henry used his blockers and went fifteen yards in the end zone for the score and a 19–14 lead with 2:24 to play in the game.

The Volunteers had a chance.

But the Tide defense rolled and sacked Tennessee quarterback Joshua Dobbs two times and forced a fumble that A'Shawn Robinson recovered to secure the 19–14 win.

Both defensive end Jonathon Allen and linebacker Ryan Anderson came through for the Alabama defense and tackled Dobbs during the drive when it mattered the most.

Day 36: Sack the Enemy

Have you ever been too weary to fight the devil? Let the Lord go to battle for you and break through the defense to sack the enemy. Allow God to come through at the right moment.

> Be watchful, stand firm in the faith, act like men, be strong. —1 Corinthians 16:13

FAITH AND PRIDE

Has life overwhelmed you at times? We have all been there. Have you had a situation where the other team has a chance to score and win the game and you are forced to watch? Perhaps you are tired from the fight because you don't see the results you had envisioned. Maybe you feel the odds are against you. Do you have it in you to make the defensive stand and sack the quarterback?

AND ROLL TIDE

This is when you must reach down and find the courage and strength to fight the enemy. The only goal the devil has is your complete destruction. There are times you feel alone, and that is exactly what he wants. But rest assured, you are wrong. The Lord will always rise to the occasion and lead the charge to win the game. You have the playbook and know how the game ends. Here are some suggestions you can think about when the game is on the line.

> ➤ Wear the Uniform: Jonathon Allen and Ryan Anderson did not go into the game without their helmets and pads. They were both prepared in mind and body before each contest. As believers, we need to make sure we are ready

to battle each day. Put on the helmet of salvation along with the belt of truth and the breastplate of righteousness. "Put on the whole armor of God, that you may be able to stand against the schemes of the devil" (Ephesians 6:11).

➤ Recognize the Target: The two Alabama defenders recognized a weakness in the offensive line and rushed to make the play. They did not wait and let the quarterback come to them. They saw the opportunity and acted. Be aware when the devil drops back to pass. He might disguise his actions in the form of temptation. Be ready to spot the play. "Call to me and I will answer you, and will tell you great and hidden things that you have not known" (Jeremiah 33:3).

➤ Huddle Up: Make sure you know what to do when the enemy drops back to throw. Be prepared and call your huddle each day in the Word of God and prayer. This will give you strength, and you will know your game plan for the day.

➤ Trust God to Deliver: When you are in position and ready for the play to start, take comfort that God is in the booth watching the entire play unfold. He will signal when to drop back in coverage and when to blitz and force the fumble.

➤ Celebrate the Win: Give God the praise during and after the game ends in victory. It doesn't matter if you face a first down and goal or third down and twenty-four. Trust God to give you the power to win, and worship Him with thankfulness.

Day 36: Sack the Enemy

Stay with God and take the fight to the enemy. Never be a stationary target. Always be on the move to make it harder for the devil to hit you. Break through the protection and allow the Lord to rush through for the sack.

DAY 37
MAKE THE MOST OF YOUR OPPORTUNITIES

January 11, 2016: Alabama 45, Clemson 40

Through God we shall do valiantly: for he it is that shall
tread down our enemies. —Psalm 108:13 KJV

The 2016 College Football Playoff National Championship was
one for the ages.

It pitted undefeated and number-one ranked Clemson
against number-two Alabama.

The hype was unbelievable, and the intensity was
overwhelming. It was a game-of-the-century matchup.

On Alabama's second drive, Derrick Henry broke loose
and rambled fifty yards for the touchdown and the 7–0 lead.

But Clemson countered and scored two times.

Quarterback Deshaun Watson put on a clinic on how to
avoid tacklers and weaved his way through the Alabama defense.

He threw two touchdowns to Hunter Renfrow, and the
Tigers took a 14–7 lead at the end of the first quarter.

In the second quarter, Watson's pass was picked off by Eddie
Jackson at the Clemson forty-two-yard line. That set the stage
for a Henry one-yard touchdown run to tie the game 14–14.

The Tide rolled in the third quarter when quarterback Jake Coker found O. J. Howard open for a fifty-three-yard touchdown pass and the 21–14 lead.

But Clemson responded when Watson took over and led the charge. Clemson converted on a thirty-seven-yard field goal and a one-yard touchdown run by Wayne Gallman and retook the lead 21–24.

On Alabama's first possession of the final quarter, Coker hit ArDarius Stewart for a thirty-eight-yard gain. That set up a field goal to tie the game 24–24.

The Tide rolled and surprised Clemson with an on-side kickoff, and Marlon Humphrey recovered the ball.

Coker wasted no time and found Howard for a fifty-yard touchdown and the 31–24 lead.

On the next drive, Clemson pulled to within four points when they kicked a field goal.

But the Tide stunned the Tigers when Kenyan Drake took the kickoff and went ninety-five yards for the touchdown and the 38–27 lead.

Watson countered and orchestrated an eight-play drive covering seventy-five yards that ended with a fifteen-yard touchdown pass to Artavius Scott.

But the Tide defense rolled and stopped Watson on the two-point conversion, and the Tigers trailed Bama 38–33.

On Alabama's next possession, Coker fired a screen to Howard, who bolted sixty-three yards. With less than three minutes left in the game, he ran the ball up the middle to give the Tide a first down.

Coker then converted a third down on a key scramble. Henry followed with a third-down conversion for a touchdown and the 45–33 lead.

Clemson answered with a quick drive under a minute that resulted in a twenty-four-yard touchdown strike by Watson to Jordan Leggett with twelve seconds to play.

The onside kick failed, and Bama recovered the ball and held on for the National Championship.

In spite of being outplayed by Clemson, Alabama took advantage of three key plays to pull off the win:

- The interception of Watson in the second quarter.
- The surprise onside kick early in the fourth quarter.
- The kickoff return for the touchdown in the fourth quarter.

These three plays accounted for twenty-one points.

But thanks be to God, which giveth us the victory through our Lord Jesus Christ. —1 Corinthians 15:57 KJV

FAITH AND PRIDE

Your National Championship relies on your relationship with the Lord. There are struggles, and there are moments of joy. Life is full of uncertainty. You could be on top of the world one day and jobless the next. You could return from the greatest vacation ever and receive news that your health may be in jeopardy. Or death can strike a loved one any time. How do you handle these interceptions?

AND ROLL TIDE

God never promised that you would not have to punt a few times in life. But He did give His word that you will be victorious if you play on His team. However, along the way, there will be times when the other team will score a touchdown. But if the Lord is your coach, He will call the right plays at the right times that will allow you to reach the end zone before the clock runs out.

What can you do to account for the big victory? You can pull off key plays that can help put you into the winner's circle and claim the trophy. Here are some ways you can make these plays happen:

➤ Attend Church: You cannot win the game if you don't show up at the field. Alabama would not have become National Champions without showing up at the University of Phoenix Stadium.

➤ Serve Others: When you put the needs of others in front of your own, you show humility and gratitude for your blessings. Give your time at a homeless shelter or a food pantry and lift up those who need your help. "The liberal soul shall be made fat: and he that watereth shall be watered also himself" (Proverbs 11:25 KJV).

➤ Lead by Example: Do right no matter what is at stake. If you have to sacrifice something important, then step up and make the call. God will take care of you. Let the Lord guide you as you follow your convictions, and if there is a conflict, the Master will make the call for you. Obey His will, and do what is right and just. "Learn to do well, seek judgment, relieve the oppressed, judge the fatherless, plead for the widow" (Isaiah 1:17 KJV).

➤ Become Involved: In addition to being active in church, consider involvement in a civic organization. Lend a hand in youth sports or run for a school board. Lead a Bible study or consider starting a writing ministry. There are many ways you can spread the gospel of Christ. Don't be content to stand on the sideline.

➤ Praise God Always: When you glorify the Lord, you are always a winner. "God is a Spirit: and they that worship him must worship him in spirit and in truth" (John 4:24 KJV).

What can you do to account for the big victory? You can put these key plays into action to make it to the winner's circle and claim the trophy.

DAY 38
LIVE FOR EVERY DAY

January 1, 2018: Alabama 24, Clemson 6

This is the day which the LORD hath made; we will rejoice and be glad in it. —Psalm 118:24 KJV

Alabama wanted to avenge its previous loss to Clemson, which happened in the 2017 College Football National Championship on the last play of the game. The Tide also wanted to prove they belonged in the big show because there were some rumblings from commentators and other media who questioned the pick.

Alabama had something to prove in the Sugar Bowl and the College Football Playoff National Championship semifinal game.

Both teams posted a strong defensive showing, but the Crimson Tide got on the board first when Andy Pappanastos booted a twenty-four-yard field goal midway through the first quarter.

The Tide rolled to a 10–0 lead when quarterback Jalen Hurts connected with Calvin Ridley on a twelve-yard touchdown strike.

Clemson countered in the second quarter when Alex Spence nailed a forty-four-yard field goal and closed the gap 10–3 at the half.

Alabama made a goof early in the third quarter when Hurts and running back Damien Harris mishandled the ball and fumbled. Clemson recovered, but the Bama defense was stingy and limited the Tigers to a forty-two-yard field goal to make the score 10–6.

The Tide defense again rose to the occasion, and defensive lineman Daron Payne intercepted a Clemson pass.

Alabama reached the red zone, and Coach Nick Saban sent in his tough goal line set, which included Payne as a key blocker most of the time.

However, Payne caught the Clemson defense off guard and ran out to the flat where Hurts connected with him for the touchdown and the 17–6 lead.

The play is immortalized as the "big man touchdown."

On the next possession, Alabama's Levi Wallace picked off another Tiger pass and romped into the end zone for the 24–10 lead.

Payne was named defensive co-MVP of the game.

His interception and touchdown sparked the Tide and helped him to enjoy a tremendous day on the field in New Orleans.

He lived for the moment.

> Take therefore no thought for the morrow: for the morrow shall take thought for the things of itself. Sufficient unto the day is the evil thereof. —Matthew 6:34 KJV

FAITH AND PRIDE

Do you have a deep desire to make the big play for the Lord? Do you find yourself procrastinating when you could do more? Do you let other distractions get in your way? It's easy. Life happens. You might have the best of intentions, but things pop up and demand your attention. You may have plans to visit a nursing home, but then you have to take your child to ball practice. This is just an example of how you could be pulled in different directions.

AND ROLL TIDE

You have prayed and asked the Master to show you ways you can make the big play. You want to roll out and catch the ball for the touchdown, but the devil's defense has their eyes on you. They toss interference flags in your way to cause you to lose focus. Not today. Not this play, you tell yourself. Here are some tips on how you can live for the moment:

➤ Volunteer: Do research and make a commitment to a worthwhile cause that is near and dear to your heart. You can become a Big Brother/Big Sister or give your time to a homeless shelter. Donate your time, and clean up after a high school football game. Make yourself useful, and be an example for others to follow. "Give, and it shall be given unto you; good measure, pressed down, and shaken together, and running over, shall men give into your bosom. For with the same measure that ye mete withal it shall be measured to you again" (Luke 6:38 KJV).

➤ Look Out for the Elderly: Don't take any payment for this kind and generous act. Do some outside maintenance, offer to cut grass, or clean up around their home. Treat it as though it were your own home. Lend a hand to make someone feel special.

➤ Start a Christian Ministry: This is something you can do right now, and it can be something big or something small. You might start an afterschool mentoring ministry for teenage boys, or you could send cards to others in your church who are sick or have lost loved ones. Encourage others when they are down. Get started today and spread God's Word. "Study to shew thyself approved unto God, a workman that needeth not to be ashamed, rightly dividing the word of truth" (2 Timothy 2:15 KJV).

➤ Get Political: Christians are needed in community government. We need people with high morals and character to serve in leadership positions and make the right decisions. Stand for what is good, and don't compromise your convictions. Men and women of God need to take a stand and let their voices be heard.

➤ Visit the Discouraged: When you give your time to people who need support, it means a great deal to those on the receiving end. A few minutes with a person who is lonely can lift their spirits for the next several days and know they are not forgotten. "We then that are strong ought to bear the infirmities of the weak, and not to please ourselves" (Romans 15:1 KJV).

Daron Payne made two spectacular plays and enjoyed the moment that he helped the Tide roll over Clemson. It's time for you to step up and come through in a big way. Make your stand, catch the defense off guard, and haul in the throw for the score. Payne made sure that he came prepared and was ready to play. He made a dramatic impact on both sides of the field. Step up and make a difference today.

DAY 39
HALFTIME ADJUSTMENT

January 8, 2018: Alabama 26, Georgia 23

> There is one body and one Spirit—just as you were
> called to the one hope that belongs to your call.
> —Ephesians 4:4

Alabama trailed Georgia 13–0 at the halftime of the 2018 College Football Playoff National Championship.

The Tide offense had dried up and could not put points on the board. Punter J. K. Scott made several appearances in the first half.

Something had to be done. A change was needed.

Coach Nick Saban put in the backup quarterback, Tua Tagovailoa, to begin the third quarter.

A different look and a fresh start might be the key to spark the offense.

Alabama got on the board when Tagovailoa hit Henry Ruggs for a six-yard touchdown to cut into the lead 13–7 to culminate a fifty-six-yard drive.

However, the Georgia Bulldogs responded with a touchdown of their own when Jake Fromm connected with Mecole Hardman to boost the lead to 20–7.

But the Tide offense was beginning to roll.

It picked up momentum when Raekwon Davis picked off a Fromm pass and returned it to the Georgia forty-yard line.

The interception resulted in an Andy Pappanastos forty-three-yard field goal to close the gap 20–10.

Tagovailoa proved that Coach Saban made the right call when the back-up signal caller led the Tide to a fourth quarter comeback.

A field goal with 9:24 to play was followed by a seven-yard touchdown pass from Tagovailoa to Calvin Ridley that tied the game with 3:49 to go.

With three ticks left, Pappanastos had a chance to win the game, but his kick from the thirty-six-yard line missed the mark, and the game went into overtime.

A fifty-one-yard field goal gave the Bulldogs a 23–20 lead.

After Tagovailoa was sacked for a huge sixteen-yard loss, he responded with a heroic forty-one-yard touchdown strike to DeVonta Smith to win the game.

The play will be forever remembered as "second and twenty-six."

For his efforts, the young quarterback was honored with the offensive player of the game award.

> And hope does not put us to shame, because God's love has been poured into our hearts through the Holy Spirit who has been given to us. —Romans 5:5

FAITH AND PRIDE

Perhaps you are wandering along in your Christian journey and are not happy with your progress. You thought there was more to this wonderful life, and you feel as though you are in a rut. Maybe you are dissatisfied with your job or feel as though you should be getting more out of life than what you are experiencing at the moment. Although you are happy in the Lord, you are not fulfilled, and you know God has bigger plans for you.

AND ROLL TIDE

Maybe you need to make some adjustments at the break. Perhaps it's time to reevaluate your circumstances and have the courage to make some changes in your life. Coach Saban was not pleased with how the offense performed, and he did not want the team to miss out on its chance to win the National Championship. He did not worry about hurting someone's ego. His goal was to capture the title, and he knew that a change had to be made. You can do the same thing. If you feel your life is not moving in the direction that would please the Master, go in at halftime and ask the Coach for advice. Here are some things He might suggest:

➤ A New Circle of Friends: Maybe you are hanging out with the wrong crowd, and it's dragging you down. Breaking away may be difficult to do because you don't want to offend anyone, but you must do what is best for you and your family. If God is telling you to change teammates, then you don't have much choice—unless you want to lose. "That is, that we may be mutually encouraged by each other's faith, both yours and mine" (Romans 1:12).

➤ A New Attitude: In today's fast-paced lifestyle, it can be easy to lose focus on God. This doesn't mean you have drifted away, but it could be the onset. You might find yourself complaining more about your job or your surroundings. A new attitude can turn your outlook around, but you must first recognize that it needs to change. Beef up your prayer life, read the Word, and ask God to give you a more positive point of view.

➢ New Expectations: You are a child of the King. You should know and expect the Lord is going to take care of you. But you must honor Him too. When you read His Word, pray to Him daily, attend His house, and obey His laws, He will bless you. This doesn't mean He will give you all you want, but He will supply your needs. Be happy and content knowing that the Savior will deliver for you in the clutch. Expect it to happen. "The hope of the righteous brings joy, but the expectation of the wicked will perish" (Proverbs 10:28).

➢ New Priorities: What is important to you? You might have to shift some things around if your priorities are off. God might want you to visit someone in the hospital at the same time you have plans to be on the boat or teeing off on the golf course. Recreation and leisure time are important, especially with your family. But it should never stand in the way of a blessing. Shift your focus from your needs to those of others.

➢ New Hope: If you have become complacent or take your blessings for granted, pause for a moment, step back, and find where your hope lies. It is not in your new truck or corner office or things of the world. Your hope is in Christ Jesus only. "For you, O Lord, are my hope, my trust, O LORD, from my youth" (Psalm 71:5).

Day 39: Halftime Adjustment

If you find yourself down at the halftime of your spiritual walk, reexamine your focus and priorities. You have the second half to stage the comeback and win the title.

THE CRIMSON FLOW

November 16, 1907: Alabama 6, Auburn 6

There is therefore now no condemnation for those who are in Christ Jesus. —Romans 8:1

When Alabama football started in 1892, fans and newspapers referred to them as the "varsity" or the "Crimson White."

Some media writers named them the "thin red line," which was popular in the early 1900s.

But the sports editor for the *Birmingham Age-Herald* is given the credit for the nickname known today as the Crimson Tide.

When the 1907 Iron Bowl was played in Birmingham, Auburn was favored to win the game.

The contest was played in a sea of red mud that stained Alabama's white jerseys red.

Bama held the Tigers to a 6–6 draw, and the headlines in the paper read "Crimson Tide." The players were described as a red tidal wave, and the name stuck.

But how does an elephant fit the Crimson Tide?

Twenty-three years later, another sportswriter characterized the team as "red elephants" after Alabama dominated Ole Miss 64–0.

Over the next few years, the mascot took on different forms, and the university even had a real elephant at some games.

But several seasons later, Big Al the elephant (a student in costume) debuted at the Sugar Bowl in 1980 when Bama defeated Arkansas. He is as much a part and tradition of the football team as winning a National Championship.

But getting back to the name Crimson Tide.

It's unique because most teams have a state symbol or an animal as their identification.

Alabama's slogan means the squad is red and will cover you like a huge body of water and win the game.

> For the law of the Spirit of life has set you free in Christ Jesus from the law of sin and death. —Romans 8:2

FAITH AND PRIDE

Have you been covered by the crimson tide blood of Jesus? Has the Lord changed your life and given you a reason to play harder? Perhaps you have waded out a few steps into the water. You have become used to the temperature and like what you feel. Now is the time to let God smother you with His tidal wave of love. To do this, you must dive in deep and enjoy the cool water. There is no better feeling than to allow the Lord to baptize you with His mercy and grace.

AND ROLL TIDE

Throughout this devotional, I have listed five areas to focus on in each chapter. But this final one will be different. When you become a member of God's team, you take on a wonderful identity, and serving Him comes with numerous benefits. Here are some things, just to name a few, that you can rejoice in after you have been covered by the crimson tide blood of Christ:

Day 40: The Crimson Flow

➤ Your Sins Are Forgiven: Your past has been forgotten by the Lord, and you are given a fresh half to make a comeback.

➤ Your Guilt Has Been Lifted: The weight of the world and your sins have been lifted from your shoulders

➤ You Are Set Free from the Chains of Sin: You are no longer bound and enslaved to the devil.

➤ You Won't Have to Fear Death: The next step is a journey to be with the Lord when He calls you home.

➤ You Have Joy: God has placed a song in your heart and a big smile on your face.

➤ You Have Peace: No matter what you go through, you know that God will take care of you.

➤ You Have Hope: This does not mean you will not have problems, but having God on your team is the best way to cope with difficult circumstances.

➤ You Have Love: You possess a sense of compassion and humility and want to serve others.

➤ You Can Rejoice: When you are a child of the King, you have the best reason to be happy.

➤ You Can Walk in the Spirit: You have confidence and are aware that you belong to Him.

➤ You Can Praise the Lord: Just like you cheer on the Tide, you can lift your hands and thank the Master for being good to you.

➢ You Can Find Favor with God: You have the promise that the Lord wants only the best for you and will provide your needs if you only ask.

➢ You Can Be Part of a Family: Spend your time around people who care about you and love you.

➢ You Will Have a New Perspective: What was once important will no longer be a priority. A new outlook will give you a reason to get up every day.

➢ You Are on a Winning Team: You know the outcome of the game, and you are aware that you are on the best team ever assembled. You have the best Coach. Go get on the field and perform.

There is no better life than to allow yourself to be covered by the crimson blood of the Lord. And there is nothing quite like the tradition of Alabama football.

Bama has produced legends in coaching and tremendous players who graced the fields. For many, it has become part of their lives, and that is awesome. Make sure that Christ is at the center of your life first. There is nothing wrong with cheering on Alabama football, and there is no better life than living for the Lord and being covered by His grace.

Faith and pride and Roll Tide!

ABOUT THE AUTHOR

Del Duduit is a literary agent with C.Y.L.E. and freelance writer. He is represented by Cyle Young, Hartline Literary Agency and is a member of Serious Writer Inc.

He is the author of *Buckeye Believer: 40 Days of Devotions for the Ohio State Faithful* (2018, BY Books), *Bengal Believer: 40 Who-Dey-Votions for the Cincinnati Faithful* (2019, BY Books), *Dugout Devotions: Inspirational Hits from MLB's Best,* (2019, Iron Stream Books), *First Down Devotions: Inspirations from NFL's Best* (2019, Iron Stream Books), and *Auburn Believer: 40 Days of Devotions for the Tiger Faithful* (2020, Iron Stream Books).

As a former sportswriter, he won both Associated Press and Ohio Prep Sports writing awards.

In 2016, Del began concentrating more seriously on his passion for writing and building his platform. His weekly blog appears at delduduit.com, and his posts have been retweeted to as many as five million followers through social media across the United States and in two other continents.

Del's articles have appeared in Athletes in Action, *Clubhouse Magazine,* Sports Spectrum, *The Sports Column,* One Christian Voice, *The Christian View* online magazine, and *Portsmouth Metro Magazine.* His blogs have appeared on One Christian Voice and its national affiliates across the country, on ToddStarnes.com and on Almost an Author and *The Write Conversation.*

In 2017, he was named Outstanding Author, first place in short nonfiction, and first place in inspirational at the Ohio Christian Writers Conference. He also won a first place Blue Seal Award in nonfiction at the 2018 Ohio Christian Writers

Conference. In 2019, *Buckeye Believer: 40 Days of Devotions for the Ohio State Faithful* won second place in the Selah Awards for Best Devotional at the Blue Ridge Mountain Christian Writers Conference. His book, *First Down Devotions: Inspirations from NFL's Best,* was nominated as a finalist in the devotional category for the Selah Awards.

He and his wife Angie live in Lucasville, Ohio, and attend Rubyville Community Church.

If you enjoyed this book, will you consider sharing the message with others?

Let us know your thoughts at info@ironstreammedia.com. You can also let the author know by visiting or sharing a photo of the cover on our social media pages or leaving a review at a retailer's site. All of it helps us get the message out!

Facebook.com/IronStreamMedia

Iron Stream Books, New Hope® Publishers, Ascender Books, and New Hope Kidz are imprints of Iron Stream Media, which derives its name from Proverbs 27:17, "As iron sharpens iron, so one person sharpens another."

This sharpening describes the process of discipleship, one to another. With this in mind, Iron Stream Media provides a variety of solutions for churches, ministry leaders, and nonprofits ranging from in-depth Bible study curriculum and Christian book publishing to custom publishing and consultative services. Through our popular Life Bible Study, Student Life Bible Study brands, and New Hope imprints, ISM provides web-based full-year and short-term Bible study teaching plans as well as printed devotionals, Bibles, and discipleship curriculum.

For more information on ISM and Iron Stream Books, please visit

IronStreamMedia.com

ARTWORK FOR BAMA AND SEC FANS

IF YOU LIKE THE FRONT COVER OF
BAMA BELIEVER,
CHECK OUT OTHER PRINTS BY THIS ARTIST.
ALL PRINTS ARE AVAILABLE EXCLUSIVELY FROM THE BEVELED EDGE.

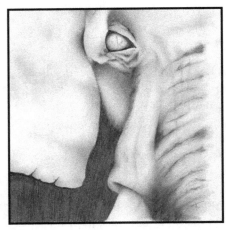

**Order a copy today at
thebevelededgeonline.com**

Search by Artist: Tim Atchenson
Search by Work: Reflections,
SEC, Alabama Prints

About the Artist

The artist, Tim Atchenson, is a twenty-eight-year veteran of the US Army and
Alabama Army National Guard. He currently serves as the supervisor for the
National Guard recruiting team based in Tuscaloosa, Alabama. He and his wife
Shannon live in the Birmingham area, and he graciously acknowledges that he
could not pursue his artistic endeavors without her support over the last
twenty-one years and counting.

9 781563 093685